DIA

GOD
IN THE
MEANTIME

A Story of Trusting God's Voice and Embracing His Timing

FOREWORD BY KWAME DAWES

Extra MILE Innovators
Kingston, Jamaica W.I.

. . . . .

Published by

Extra MILE Innovators

54 Montgomery Avenue, Kingston 10, Jamaica W.I.

www.extramileja.com

Cover Design: Joanna Klu

www.cre8tiv-arts.com

Back Cover Photo: Tito Herrera

info@titoherrera.com

Author Contact

For feedback and speaking engagements, contact the author at

gitmt2020@gmail.com

NOTES

Disclaimer

Endorsements

"It's a great book, this testimony of God's faithfulness. It reads like a conversation, authentic, engaging, serious and yet funny."

—Anthea Henderson, PhD.
Writer, Researcher, Educator
Caribbean School of Media and Communication,
The University of the West Indies, Mona

. . . . . .

"A wonderful account told with energy, wit, an engaging voice, and a clear and persistent faith in God."

—Josett Peat
Retired Professor of English
Miami Dade College

. . . . . .

"I love to read, so I have quite a collection of books. I keep most of them in my office at the church, but a few of my favorites I keep at home. Not many of the books that I read make the cut to be kept at home, but this one definitely did. I read the whole book in one sitting. I couldn't put it down. And that just might happen to you, too. Thanks, Diane, for adding another book to my special home collection. You have an amazing story. To God be the glory!"

—*Stephen Gunn*
Pastor at Crossroads Bible Church
Panama City, Panama

To my children Jonathan, Jason, and Jovanna.
Here on purpose. Here for purpose.
You were worth the wait. The world is waiting...
(Romans 8:19)

To my husband, Selwyn, I loved you before I knew it.
I'm happy GOD chose you for me.
And you're cute and funny. What more could a girl
want? Well...there's... Just kidding!
I hope we keep making youngsters realize that experienced love is the real hot stuff.

To Nathan Baldwin Thompson (Daddy T)
and
Dr. Mertel Elizabeth Thompson (Mummy T).
I love you both. You set the standard and left a legacy
for which I am eternally grateful.

To Aba, 1960-2018. I have no words...

To my AVM Awareness family, by GOD's grace we are
survivors. Nobody fights alone.

Foreword

One of the great gifts of literature is the way it can, when well written, and when it manages to find a point of emotional and intellectual relevance for the reader, transport you into another place and into fresh ways of seeing and understanding the world. Diane Batchelor's *GOD IN THE MEANTIME*, is special to me because it achieves that peculiarly compelling feat of sharpening my recollection of experiences that actually shaped and defined my life. We were at the University of the West Indies at the same time, and one of her key chapters in this work is someone close to me, my late sister Aba Polson. So, I have to admit that I was positively disposed to want to read this work and to enjoy it.

And I did enjoy it greatly. Yet the tone, the style, the enthusiastic relish in storytelling, literary traits that Diane Batchelor shows in the retelling of memory, are clear indications that this book will resonate with many people, even those who will be introduced to this world and

Batchelor's eventful life for the first time. This is a work of faith, a work that seeks to ground its raison d'etre in the expression of this faith as a lived and real thing. Batchelor's fascination with the "mean time" is a fascination with the biblical notions of "waiting," the core principle of faith which is sharpened and made relevant in the face of contending with the unseen and hoped for.

In story after story, Batchelor does not lose sight of this mission. But she is guided by a principle that those of us who are reading this work will appreciate. She has an innate understanding that the idea of being a witness is inextricably tied to the idea of chronicling, and the act of chronicling is the act of storytelling. Batchelor loves to tell a story, and every lesson, every truth, every moment of doubt, confusion, fear or loss, is told through stories, anecdotes, and remembrances, and in the end, we arrive at the sense of this woman as someone desperate to explain that her life has been guided by and shaped by her faith in God, her belief in the Bible and her rootedness in the community of believers.

So, yes, this is a work of faith. But it is also a story about a woman's journey through life—her emergence as an adult, as a professional, as mother, as a leader in the world, and as a black woman from the Caribbean living in the wider world. This book gives us a case study of the strength and beauty of such a life.

In the end, one is never in doubt about the urgency and the necessity of this telling. It is driven by a profound and vital sense of gratitude, and yes, by something more, by the desire to find some security in the framing of one's varied experiences in life around the faith belief that there is a purpose to it all, there is value to it all. Diane Batchelor believes this fully, and in the end, she writes with such power and grace that we are also compelled to believe this as well.

I am grateful to her for this book. Some of it is deeply personal. Seeing so many of the people I met and grew to love while I was an undergraduate at the University of the West Indies and after, has been a tremendous joy. I am also extremely grateful to her for finally explaining the madness of her quite speedy marriage to Selwyn. And to see the beauty and tenderness of her relationship with my sister Aba, is touching to me. But much of my gratitude goes beyond the personal. It expands to my long-held view that our lives are shaped by and defined by the ways in which we remember, the ways in which we share our remembrances and our capacity to show empathy through the act of imagining the world through language. Finally, she stands as a witness willing to share the truths of God's providence and power, and for me, this represents a blessing, a rich and bountiful blessing. Diane Batchelor's book is a splendid gift, and I assure you it is a rollicking read, and one I happily recommend.

—Kwame Dawes

Emmy Award Winning Author

Co-Founder of the Calabash International Literary Festival, Lincoln, Nebraska

Preface

Some years ago, it began to dawn on me that most times when I came across the phrase "in the meantime," it would refer to a time in which something unpleasant was taking place. Maybe it was just my imagination, but I was beginning to form an association. The period "in the meantime" came to denote a hard time - usually a time of waiting.

So, as I facilitated many women's Bible studies over the years, I began to use the phrase "When we see 'In the meantime', it is usually a mean time." I admit it's not a sophisticated way of phrasing it, but it worked for me. It helped me to understand and accept that while we wait, GOD may appear to be mean.

I'm a mom who has heard from my children the phrase, "You're being mean!" a fair bit. Sometimes they were right. But most times I was just doing my job. My job was to train, guide, and direct them (often towards goals they didn't even know they had). Until they owned their own dream, my prodding them towards, or steering them away from a particular end, in their minds appeared to be mean.

Thankfully, we grow. And it is, as I have grown and my children have also grown, that we've come to appreciate the value of the "mean times." I've even been fortunate enough to receive a few thanks for things that at first were soundly rejected.

My children have been a mirror for me reflecting back my own attitudes to my HEAVENLY FATHER. How often I have whined or thrown temper tantrums over things that, looking back, were so much for my own benefit and happiness even.

My goal in writing this is to help you avoid some of the mistakes I have made in my "mean times." But most of all it's to encourage you to not lose hope. HE who promised is faithful. If HE is making you wait, you can be assured that there is purpose in your pain.

May you find nuggets of hope in my journey. And may you experience peace in the mean time.

Prologue

By the time you hold this book in your hand, I will have become a "queenager" with quite a few "wisdom highlights" dotting my hair. (Thanks, Facebook for those gems.) That means I will have attained the grand old age of 60. It seems that this is literally an earth-stopping event. The year? 2020—the year the world stopped.

I have vivid memories of my 5-year-old self, lying in bed trying to imagine an older me. I mentally clambered up the stairs of the foreseeable years till I arrived at the massively enormous number 20. Having ventured so very far, the tiny legs of my young imagination gave way. Could there really be life after that great, big, humongous, Jack-and-the-Beanstalk giant number? Childhood naiveté; you've gotta love it!

I still recall my midlife crisis. I turned 25.

Twenty-five was such an old age!

I had reached a half of 50! A quarter century!

My life was almost over!

Suddenly, I hit 40.

Strangely, it was then that I began to feel so young and full of life. I couldn't understand why 40 had seemed so very out of my reach, so very old. Forty was the new twenty, fifteen even. I was young, alive and more at home with myself than I had ever been. Getting older did have its benefits after all. With this new mindset, I have proceeded to embrace the years.

Sixty is a milestone. And for me it's even more so, because at 57 my life almost ended. As I have thought about ways to celebrate this pinnacle, to mark this Ebenezer moment, this point when I can clearly say "hitherto has the Lord helped me" (1Samuel 7:12 KJV), I have decided to record just a few of the many instances in my journey in which I have had to clap my hand over my mouth and go "Whoa! Look at GOD!"

These "memorial stone moments" have usually come in connection with a "mean time"—those years of waiting to see things unfold—the "meantime" of waiting. It is as Jay and Katherine Wolf put it so well, "The space between our expectations and realities... where our disappointment lies." I call those times my "mean times."

Telling these life stories is recounting some of the loving deeds of the Lord along my journey to making peace with disappointment. It highlights a loving GOD at work in the meantime. If you're going through a "mean time," I pray these 60 Chapters plus a brawta (bonus) from my journey may help you find HIS peace.

"One generation shall praise Your works to another, and shall declare Your mighty and remarkable acts" (Psalms 145:4, AMP).

CONTENTS

PART ONE

Small Beginnings

So, when you have stories to tell—GOD stories, where do you begin?

In the beginning.

Crawling on hands and knees as a young child, I climbed the seemingly vertical hill to the tiny house where I was born. I remember the sheets of newspaper and magazine pages that lined the walls. How did I come to be born in such a tiny, dark room in the hills of Jamaica in a Maroon town called Accompong? Yes, that made me Maroon.

I am the second of my mom's five children. My older brother, born in a hospital, came so easily that my mom thought this was to be a pattern for all of her deliveries. Being a student-teacher, young wife of a young student-pastor in the hills of St Elizabeth, she quickly agreed to the local midwives' offer of helping her deliver her second child—me. Well, let's just say, she never did that again. I have the (dubious?) honor of being the only one of her five offspring to be born at home. This leads me to another birth story many years later—almost 37 to be exact. But I run way ahead of myself.

I did mention my dad was a pastor, yes? It also made me JESUS' cousin or some closely related next of kin. I joke—but barely. I grew up with a sense of innate goodness that made me feel the call to the altar to accept JESUS was for other folks—the sinners—not me. It was not until a summer camp as an almost 13-year old, that I finally became aware of my own need for a savior. That savior, JESUS, soon became my Best Friend with whom I shared the deepest secrets and desires of my heart.

So, I began my tale with my young parents' starting their family. Let's go back there. My dad used to boast that he was very happy to have started his family at a young age, so he could grow up with his children. Being somewhat a daddy's girl, I cottoned on to that dream and made it my own. My parents married when my mom was 22. I admired my mom, so that also became my goal. As with everything dear to my heart, I shared this desire with my

Best Friend. HIS Word says, if my ways pleased HIM, HE would grant me the desires of my heart. So, I tried hard to please HIM, and made sure HE knew my heart's desires. Here they were, I would:

Marry early

Start a family

Grow up with my children.

Who settles for one out of three? Not me.

I did get married at 22. And to a man GOD hand-picked (now that's a story!) But what about the children of my youth? First comes love, then comes marriage, then comes...

Again, I run ahead of myself.

And so, It Begins

You see, somewhere in my teenage years, I learned that crushes revealed could ruin friendships. I also learned that having a platonic relationship could be so much less stressful. Added to that, being the second child and oldest girl in my Jamaican family, I felt very much like I was the first child and had the most responsibility. My older brother may protest, but this is my story. Clearly, I had a deep yearning for a big brother. Sorry Donny, but one year older in the same family doesn't count, especially when my parents declared that I was born older than my years—a blessing and a curse. So, facing the stresses of life during my first year at the University of the West Indies (UWI), I pleaded with GOD for this brother to whom I could pour out my heart with no strings attached.

In the strangest of ways, GOD answered my prayer. I started having a crush on one of the brothers in my friend group. I knew him well enough to know we were never meant to be. This put a strain on our friendship and caused me to descend into a funk. Coincidentally, the other women in our friend group seemed to be in the same state.

Our small prayer group frequently met in the Old Works Farmhouse, an abandoned building in the university's Chapel Gardens. One night we divided up, and each of the brothers paired up with a sister to try to get to the bottom of what was ailing us. I prayed frantically, "Please GOD, not that stoic, super-spiritual guy. He would never understand the crazy roller coaster that is my young-girl's heart." Suffice it to say, after we were paired up, I was distraught. Why?

Some years before, two young men arrived at my high school. One was short and dark. One was tall and caramel colored. During their two years at St Jago High School, I discovered they both sang well. In fact, we all sang to-gether in our school's glee club.

Over time the tall one gave his heart to the LORD and, joined his friend as part of our school's Inter-Schools Christian Fellowship (ISCF) group. He would also come occasionally to the weekly youth worship gatherings our family's Friday evening devotions had become.

Despite all this interaction, I had absolutely no interest in this caramel-colored, six-footer. He struck me as stoic. And to tell the truth, I also preferred darker men. So, now you can imagine my distress when I found myself across from him that night!

3

Things Are Not Always What They Seem

Folks always say, "GOD has a sense of humor." Well, I was becoming the butt of HIS joke. We had agreed to honestly share with whomever we were paired, so I took a deep breath and dove right in, my underarms dripping my embarrassment. I blurted out my shame and waited for the judgment to begin.

To my utter amazement, he listened compassionately and then floored me by sharing that he himself was facing a similar dilemma. Soon we were tripping over each other comparing our stories and giving each other advice. Whoa! Talk about a very pleasant surprise!

When our allotted time to share was up, we both agreed to meet at another time to continue to help each other over our separate hurdles of the heart. By the time we had gotten together a few times, I was overwhelmed with gratitude to GOD. I knew my prayer for a brother had been answered. And from the most unlikely of sources! Go GOD!

In short order, we were inseparable. I could finally pour out my heart to another human without judgment and with no strings attached. And he was the best listener! I was in heaven!

That is till the day he asked to meet with me in one of the students' lounges, Mary Seacole Hall's Common Room.

4

Don't Mess with Success

When I entered the room, he was already there seated in a corner. When he stood to greet me, his eyes took on a warm glow, as they flickered over me, coming to rest just above my eyes. His words came softly, "You look very nice. I like your hair pinned up high like that."

"Thank you." I responded, smoothing my skirt and sitting in the chair diagonal to his. His eyes had now come to look searchingly into mine. What was that look in his eyes? Involuntarily, I squirmed at the strange new sensation in my tummy. Were those butterflies? What on earth! Was he falling for me? Or worse, was I falling for him? Just what I needed.

Before I could gather my thoughts, he was telling me how much he was beginning to desire a deeper relationship with me. No! I treasured this new friendship too much to watch it be spoilt by a silly crush. I would have to rescue it myself.

As soon as he stopped talking, I countered with my winning argument. Of course, he would think he was in love with me. We got along so very well, and we genuinely liked each other. But that's to be expected in a great male-female relationship. If we would just give it time, these feelings would pass, and we would revert to the awesome brother-sister relationship we shared.

Selwyn appeared to see the logic in my argument. I was not going to lose my new-found, best-friend-brother to a silly crush, and that was that.

5

The Tables Turn

Just about that time on our university campus, a new phenomenon was surfacing. There were people approaching others and telling them they were sure GOD had said they should be married. I was totally affronted by this presumption, and I had a plan for anyone who dared approach me with such self-serving nonsense. As much as I enjoyed a close relationship with the LORD, I did not believe HE told people whom they should marry.

So, there I was in Chancellor Hall one morning kneeling with Selwyn at his bedside in prayer over some matter of mutual concern, when it happened. I had a strong sense that GOD was speaking to me!

Blood pumping so fast I could hear its buzzed sloshing in my ears, I distinctly heard GOD speak to my heart. What would I do? It seemed to be a message for us both. As I wrestled in my mind, and my armpits once again became a fountain, I heard Selwyn say, "Speak LORD." I felt caught with no way out than to confess what I believed GOD had told me.

Stalling for time, I broke from prayer mode to ask in a voice thickened by fear, "Do you believe GOD is saying something?" As my mind raced for a door of escape, the response was, "We will see."

With the little time the response allowed, I came up with a plan to edit and explain away what I had heard. After all, what self-respecting young woman tells a man she believes GOD had brought them together? He seemed to have bought my interpretation that our being brought together was as brother and sister. With that, I hastily retreated from his room.

Although I was thankful that I had avoided a very awkward situation, I knew what I had heard. And that did not give me one drop of relief. After sorting out my thoughts and acknowledging that I did have romantic feelings for him, I soon realized that I had been so focused on maintaining a platonic relationship that I must have buried any attraction I had begun to feel. I finally found solace in planning to, next time, accept when he came again to declare his love.

For it stood to reason that GOD, being a gentleman, would speak clearly to him, and he would in turn come to me, and I would then graciously accept. Neatly packaged and tied with a bow, as things should be. I would wait.

Our friendship changed for me that day. I had seen GOD's intentions, and I was now impatient to have it out in the open, so we could get on with our lives. But nothing was happening.

In the meantime, Selwyn kept being my brother-friend with not so much as a word about GOD telling him I was to be his. With every chance, I badgered GOD to do the right thing and let Selwyn come to me.

Finally, one day HE answered. HIS desire was for me to go to Selwyn and tell him clearly what I had known all along and had tried to explain away. There was no way I could do that. I begged to be released.

In the end, I decided I would write it. I would give him the letter and then run as far away as my shaking legs would take me.

6

Dreams and Schemes

S o, the next day we met in our usual spot in the university's Chapel Gardens. But, before I gave him the note, I came up with my final, sure-to-succeed, marvelously brilliant plan. This was genius. Here's how it went:

Me:	Selwyn, I've been thinking about our friendship...
Selwyn:	Yes?
Me:	And it's dawned on me that we spend a lot of time together...
Selwyn:	Yes?

Me:	Well, I just think that if GOD had some-one for each of us, we probably wouldn't even notice, because we're so caught up in each other's lives.
Selwyn:	So?
Me:	Maybe we should take a break. Give each other some space. Give ourselves the chance to see who GOD may have in mind for us.

This was the epitome of my master plan. This was the point where he was supposed to fall to his knees and declare that he knew GOD had planned for us to have a future together as man and wife.

As I prepared to graciously accept GOD's plan, (cue the birds twittering overhead, the soft breeze rustling the leaves, and the violins softly playing), he said,

"Yes, I think you are right. It's a good idea to give each other some space."

Suddenly, someone drew a fingernail across the chalk-board of my dreams.

The violins hit the most discordant note.

The breeze violently sucked the breath from my body.

I was left in a daze, but trying desperately to carry on with the script that I had written.

I had no choice but to pretend that this was exactly what I had desired.

7

The Thing I Feared Most

We retreated for the last time from our usual meeting place in the garden. He, to a life in which he was encouraged to open his eyes in case his future bride was in sight, and me to the refuge of my friend's dorm room, where I bawled my eyes out.

It had happened. I had lost my best friend. As I wailed before GOD for days, the scripture that surfaced to taunt me was Job's declaration that, "The thing I feared most has come upon me" (Job 3:25 paraphrased).

Cold! Was this how JESUS, my true Best Friend was treating me?

For a whole year, Selwyn and I did the awkward dance of those who once were really close friends and had become polite strangers. It was bizarre.

In the meantime, my relationship with GOD also took on a different flavor. I was now forced to confront my doubts about HIS speaking into the details of one's life.

For a whole year I watched, as Selwyn showed interest in other women, while I was bound by what I knew GOD had revealed to me. It was also the year in which GOD painstakingly taught me to hear HIS voice. I still recall this as one of the most profound and tender lessons of my life. GOD had a purpose for this mean time.

Learning to Listen

Remember my disdain for people declaring that GOD had specifically directed them? Well, quite a bit of that was based on my fear of being led astray and deceived by the Devil. After all, how many twisted murderers have claimed that "god" had told them to do it?

When I finally opened myself to hearing from GOD, it was on the assurance that HE would not allow me to be deceived. "My sheep hear my voice..." (John 10: 27). With not a little trepidation, I embarked on a journey of learning to hear HIS voice.

It began in the simplest of ways. I would be heading to my friend's dorm room at a time when I knew she had a break in her classes and was usually there. I would hear a clear, "She's not there." Doubting that the impression was the voice of GOD, I would head there anyway. Sure enough, she wouldn't be there. "Must be a fluke." I told myself.

On another occasion when I knew for sure she shouldn't be there, I would hear clearly, "Go now. She's there." Timidly I would obey, and there she'd be. Hmm, slowly but surely, I was beginning to allow myself to be led by GOD's voice.

An instance that stands out for me was when I had the strong impression to go to a friend's room and give her the princely sum of five dollars. Still trying to be certain this was GOD, I went to her room and engaged in small talk aimed at discerning whether or not she was in fact in need.

After a few minutes of pleasant conversation, I said my goodbyes and headed down the hallway. I had not gone very far, when the distinct voice of GOD spoke firmly to me, "Go give her five dollars!" At this point I was exasperated, so I spun around and blurted from her open door, "What do you need five dollars for?"

My poor friend, caught totally off-guard, responded that she had run out of meal tickets and needed money to buy dinner from the campus Soda Fountain. After fishing the bill from my pocket and handing it to her, I again walked down the corridor.

This time I was overwhelmed by a sense of GOD's awesomeness that would stoop to be intimately interested in such a small matter as my friend's dinner that evening. In making sure she had dinner, HE was also teaching me a valuable lesson. I could trust HIS voice.

After a while, I began to liken the experience of knowing GOD's voice to being able to recognize the voice of a frequent telephone caller. At first, you may need to ask the person to identify himself or herself. However, after many conversations, you find no need for that. You have instant voice recognition.

And so, it was in my journey of hearing GOD's voice. HE also led me through the Bible, the voice of trusted leadership, and circumstantial confirmation. Being able to recognize HIS voice kept me during the mean time. Eventually, I was to meet someone whose words became the voice of GOD that changed my life.

9

A Man of Integrity

In 1980 during my first year at the University of the West Indies, I had the life-changing privilege of becoming joined to a group of singers and musicians who would eventually become the award-winning New Creation band.

During the year of watching Selwyn check out other prospects, I also began to let my affections roam. As I poured out my heart to one of the brothers in our band, I found myself entertaining the idea that maybe I should move on. Maybe I should forget about Selwyn.

After all, he hadn't even been my original idea of what my husband would look like. And this new confidant was also returning the strong feelings I began to feel for him. Maybe Selwyn's time had passed.

But GOD, HE doesn't let you wander, not if your heart is truly set to obey HIM. So, despite my reasoning with HIM to let me off the hook and allow me to pursue other love interests, HE was unrelenting. HIS word to me was that I was as married to Selwyn, as if I had his ring on my finger and the marriage certificate in my bedside drawer.

My brother in the band also knew what GOD had spoken to me. So, together we committed to supporting each other to be obedient to GOD above all. He helped me devise ways to avoid closeness with him without causing the rest of the group to feel uncomfortable. We had all by then become such a close-knit family, that people avoiding one another would have been terribly obvious.

It is still one of the best examples I have of what a godly man can do to honor GOD. He committed to praying for my strength to obey GOD's word to me, and I prayed that GOD would honor his faithfulness by providing him with a godly wife.

10

The Divine Meddler

It was the summer of 1981. Our singing group had recently accepted spiritual oversight from one Capt. Raphael Mason, an officer in the Salvation Army and a leader in the Deeper Life Ministries Charismatic Movement in Jamaica.

Being the effervescent, take-charge, people-person he always was, he immediately set up a string of individual appointments aimed at getting to know the group better. Soon it was my turn to meet him, so I made my way to his office at the headquarters of the Salvation Army on the busy Waterloo Road.

It didn't take Raphael long to break through my introvert defenses and open me up to easy conversation. Shortly before my time with him was up, he asked a very personal question—was I in a romantic relationship with anyone? I told him I wasn't.

Raphael expressed surprise and proceeded to pry further. Was there no one at all in the picture? Finally, I confessed what had happened the year before, when I felt the LORD had told me to tell Selwyn HE had brought us together, and I had refused to do it.

Raphael took on an air of seriousness and declared, "If I were your shepherd (a then Charismatic term for pastor), I would send you right now to speak to him." I laughed uncomfortably and thought, "Well, you're not my shepherd, so you certainly can't make me do any such thing!" With that I bade him goodbye and headed home.

I chuckled to myself all through the 40 minutes by bus that it took from the bustling Waterloo Road to my quiet, tree-lined neighborhood of College Commons. My good friend, Denise, greeted me, as I walked by her front gate.

During our chit-chat, I casually mentioned the crazy thing this fool-fool (a Jamaican phrase for crazy) man had suggested. We both had a good belly laugh. However, as I was about to leave her gate to continue my walk home, she sobered up and asked, "But suppose that's what GOD wants you to do?" Now I wasn't laughing so easily. She had shaken my confidence.

I arrived home totally unnerved. While trying to push this absurd idea out of my mind, I opened my bedside drawer. Out fell a carefully folded letter. Curious, I picked it up and unfolded it. I was surprised to see my own handwriting. As I began to read, my mouth fell open. I stood transfixed.

It was the letter!

The letter I had written the year before.

The letter telling Selwyn what I believed GOD had said.

The letter I had planned to give to him that day.

The letter I had written before I had suddenly changed the plan.

The letter I had kept in my hand.

The letter—stark evidence of the day my scheming had backfired.

I was shaking.

GOD was indeed trying to tell me something. This time I would have to obey.

Looking back, I wish the letter had survived the years. It may have saved me from other instances of foolishly trying to manipulate GOD.

If I Perish

I spent the rest of my summer holidays preparing for the inevitable. I was a woman on death row. Like Esther and Jephthah's daughter, I fasted and prayed and asked a few key friends to fast and pray with me. This time I would do as I had been told, and if I perished, I perished.

D-Day for me was the first week of the new school year. Finally, and too soon, it arrived.

Bolstered by the prayers of my close sister-circle, lead-footed, I trudged up the stairs to Selwyn's dorm room on Block A Chancellor Hall.

My knocks on his door sounded in my head like a judge's gavel. I was the fear-drained convict waiting for my executioner. After what seemed like an eternity, I finally grasped that no one was home.

I let out the breath I hadn't realized I had been holding and thought I had escaped. Maybe, like Abraham, GOD was just testing my faith to see if I would be obedient this time. My reprieve, my ram in the thicket, was his not being there. I was free again! I turned to sprint down the stairs.

However, I felt impressed to leave a note to say I had been there, and where I would be if he did want to contact me. Not exactly what I had had in mind, but still way better than what had lain ahead of me. I quickly scribbled the note and headed back to Mary Seacole Hall. I would go hang out in my friend's room and calm my frayed nerves. I did not expect to see him that day.

It's amazing how stress can make you tired! On my way to my friend's room, I was greeted from the open room door of another friend, Marva, who invited me in. In short order, after chatting for a bit, I was soon sprawled across her bed fast asleep. I awoke some hours later and finally made it to my original destination.

I would at last be able to release my pent-up emotions and fill my friends in on how I had dodged the bullet. I opened the door without knocking and was in turn nearly knocked off my feet in fright. There, seated at the desk, writing into a notebook, was none other than the ruggedly handsome Selwyn Batchelor!

He had found my note, skipped some lectures, and had for over three hours been waiting where I had said I would be. I was trapped. This time there was no way out.

Here I was once again sitting across from my best-friend brother—the one with whom I used to feel free to be my truest self. This time his presence was not reassuring. Quite the contrary, it was terrifying.

My mind raced back to the day when he had sat opposite me declaring his growing feelings for me. That's how it should have been—him asking me. How did I get to be the one about to make a complete fool of myself? After all, wasn't it fools who walked around telling people, "GOD said...?" Well, today that fool was me. I was going to lay it all out there. GOD had said.

Going out on a limb,

taking a leap of faith,

jumping off the proverbial cliff,

preparing to hit rock bottom,

I blurted it out.

"I believe GOD told me you are to be my husband."

Cue the eternity of stunned silence.

12

Shameless Hussy

ut the silence was short-lived. Emboldened by my doing the most shameful thing I could imagine, and knowing that having hit the bottom there was nowhere to go but up, I continued to pour out the whole story. What I had heard GOD say—exactly what HE said this time—no omissions, no interpretations.

A peace came over me—a relief at finally having been obedient to GOD's voice. Along with that was a strong assurance that this was not my fight.

Selwyn's response was way more gracious than mine would have been, though he asked the same question of me:

"How did I know that this was GOD and not just my emotions?"

A very fair question indeed.

And I had asked myself that question a million times during the past year of our awkward interactions. That year had given me time to honestly confront myself. It also gave me the chance to settle it with GOD.

In fact, I had spent that summer searching the Scriptures, listening to wise counsel (thanks Rawle!), and searching my own heart. I came to the conclusion that yes; Selwyn Batchelor had stolen my heart. But way more than the warm flush, quickened heartbeat, and butterflies in my tummy that his nearness evoked, was a quiet assurance that GOD had a joint plan for our lives.

But there was no need for Selwyn to feel pressure from me. I was now embarking on a trusting relationship with GOD. If HE had indeed spoken, it was up to HIM to bring HIS word to pass.

And I told Selwyn so. He could feel free to avoid me. I certainly would have avoided him if the shoe had been on the other foot. I reassured him that I expected nothing from him. I just needed to be obedient to what GOD was leading me to do. With that, I planned to stay clear out of his way.

But as a good friend of mine had the habit of saying, "Man ah plan, an' GOD ah wipe out!" (Now there's a

Jamaican proverb for you!). In other words, "Many are the plans in a person's heart, but it is the LORD's purpose that prevails" (Proverbs 19:21 New International Version NIV).

Little did I know that, in absentia, I had been selected to work on the same Intervarsity Christian Fellowship (IVCF) committee that Selwyn, as Vice-President that year, chaired. This committee held weekly planning meetings. And guess where we would regularly convene? In Selwyn's dorm room! So much for making myself scarce and avoiding him.

With time, having had to face both my biggest fear and my biggest shame at once, I eventually settled into a routine of practicing obedience to GOD, even when it felt silly. And it certainly felt silly.

Ever so often the LORD would have me pray specific prayers for Selwyn and then have me write a message from HIM concerning the matter. At first, I would scan Selwyn's face, desperately needing some confirmation that I was truly being led by GOD. No confirmation came. He would take the note, politely thank me, and that was that. I was to have no reassurance from anyone but GOD.

13

Giver of Dreams

That was also the period when I freely complained and poured out my doubts to GOD. As much as I knew in my heart what HE had told me, and as much as I knew of my own longing for Selwyn, the situation seemed destined for failure.

Even though I had often been accused of being a "Pollyanna," I could also be pragmatic. So, with no encouragement coming from Selwyn except the occasional furtive glance, I was prepared to let it go. I would not fall into the trap of reading too much into the slightest gesture, as some were doing.

One day as I poured out my complaint (sounds spiritual, eh? Plainly put, I was whining), GOD led me to the book of Jeremiah and answered me as clearly as if HE had stood before me in conversation. Chapter 33 has never again been the same to me.

This is what the Lord says: *You have said, 'This is a desolate land* where people and animals have all disappeared.' Yet in the empty streets of Jerusalem and Judah's other towns, *there will be heard once more the sounds of joy and laughter. The joyful voices of bridegrooms and brides will be heard again*, along with the joyous songs of people bringing thanksgiving offerings to the Lord. They will sing, 'Give thanks to the Lord of Heaven's Armies, for the Lord is good. His faithful love endures forever!' For *I will restore the prosperity of this land to what it was in the past,* says the Lord.

This is what the Lord says: *If you can break my covenant with the day and the night so that one does not follow the other, only then will my covenant* with my servant David *be broken*. Only then will he no longer have a descendant to reign on his throne. The same is true for my covenant with the Levitical priests who minister before me." (Jeremiah 33:10-11, 20-21 New Living Translation NLT emphasis mine)

It was from these verses that God emphasized to me how settled HIS word was. If I could break the covenant of night and day, then HIS word would not come to pass. I knew I couldn't break that covenant, but still I entertained doubts.

One night I had a very clear dream. I was in Selwyn's dorm room. He was apologizing for seeming to shut me out, and I was reassuring him that I harbored no hard feelings. I assured him it was all the work of the LORD, and that I was OK with it. It was so real! I woke up and quickly wrote it down. It was January 28, 1982.

On the night of February20, it came to pass. That was the night I took him the birthday gift I had made for him — the craft project the LORD had told me to give to him, since it was my favorite, and one day it would hang in my own home.

That night Selwyn confessed that he was feeling like he had hurt me by his actions and asked for my forgiveness. I reassured him that, strangely enough, I didn't feel he had any reason to apologize and that this journey I was on was really a GOD thing. It all boiled down to what HE was doing in my life.

You see, at that point, probably more than any other point in my life, I had become acutely aware that it was truly the MOST HIGH who rules in the affairs of men. Nothing, absolutely nothing that happened in my life was not permitted by GOD. And if HE permitted it, it was for a very good reason, and it was certainly for my best. And I told Selwyn so. (Funny how I have kept repeating that lesson. Like a house that never stays clean, I have needed to relearn this over the years.)

It seemed like this was the key needed to unlock the prison door behind which Selwyn had been guarding his emotions. Almost in a flash, our old friendship returned. We were again Selwyn and Diane, best friends laughing and talking freely. It was just like I had dreamt it.

14

The Brown Suede Jacket

As we stood up from the edge of his little twin bed to make the short walk over to my friend's place, our friendship again changed in an instant.

He was putting on the brown suede jacket his dad had left when he had returned to England, his home of many years. In fact, Selwyn was born there, had come to Jamaica with his mom and younger sister at three years old, and had lived most of his life without his dad.

He had met him at ten years old when one day, without any prior notice, he showed up at the house in which the family was then living. Selwyn recalls his mom pointing to the strange man and saying, "This is your father." He had stayed for a few months, and then had returned to his home in London, England.

Selwyn was finally able to solve the mystery of the peculiar blue envelopes that would appear in his mother's room ever so often. This was the man who had been sending them. The man was his father.

His father, Onis Batchelor, returned some years later, having declared that he would come to build his family a home. And so he did. He stayed the many months it took to build a house from scratch. He had gathered a team of workers and became his own architect, builder, and con-tractor. For him this was not a mammoth task. As he proudly informed his son, he was one of the men who had erected the BBC tower in London.

Mission accomplished, after a few years, he returned to his work in London. But he left a few things behind. One of these was his brown suede jacket. It was the auburn color of the cow on which my grandpa had propped me as a child. It was a tawny, buttery soft mantle that swallowed Selwyn's meager frame.

As he slipped into it to shield himself from the cool night air we were about to enter, I suddenly found myself caught in an embrace. It was our first. And although it caught me completely off guard, there was no fear. It was as if I had finally come home.

I nuzzled the softness and fragrance of the oversized jacket and allowed myself to bask in the rightness of the moment. GOD was truly a miracle worker. I had my friend back!

But better yet, if that dream had so quickly come to pass, I knew without a doubt that everything else GOD had told me would become reality. This lovely man was without a doubt my husband!

That night I whispered, "I love you."

15

By Accident

Eventually, things began to change. Selwyn would just happen to be seated under the spreading rubber tree in the university's Arts Faculty. This majestic tree had roots that traversed the breadth of the Faculty's open area and seemed to draw us into community under its shade.

Somehow, Selwyn would appear there conveniently at a time when my classes were out. He would also somehow leave all the vendors stationed in the Science Faculty (his faculty) in order to purchase his midday meal from the Arts' vendor who commandeered a corner of the parking lot. Before long, it became clear that our frequent accidental meetings were no accident.

In fact, before I knew it, he would be accompanying me all the way home to my Liguanea residence. It was on one of those evenings that he confessed that he still had strong feelings for me and believed I would be his wife.

With that he pulled me in and planted a passionate kiss on my lips. That kiss sealed the deal. We were finally in a relationship.

16

The Concert

W e were so engrossed in headily making up for lost time, that we both forgot that I was supposed to be ministering with my group, New Creation, at a concert that very Friday evening. While he waited for me, I hastily got dressed in my band uniform and we bolted to the venue.

This particular event was somewhat of a full circle. You see, the group's very first official concert was held the year before— the year when our friendship had changed. It was the year in which I had suggested he take the time to look around for who GOD may have for him as a wife. And look around he did!

I'll take you back there, so you see for yourself the completed circle.

Let me paint you the picture of a well-painted girl (me in makeup for the first time, and I dare say it was very heavily done) blinking out into the audience as the curtain rose or parted (I can't recall which), to have her eyes adjust and settle on a cute couple seated in the very front row. That couple was Selwyn and a lovely young lady who was his date that night.

It was the Ward Theatre—a gem of a building, full of architectural glory and replete with the rich heritage of Jamaican creative greatness. This was the esteemed venue for our very first, real concert. How fortunate we were to have been invited to sing in such a treasure!

We had worked hard to make ourselves worthy of the gift. We stepped up our rehearsals. We made ourselves shiny silver-grey outfits. And we enlisted the wife of the main performer, Dennis Malcolm, to transform us into beings worthy of such an illustrious stage.

And transform she did. Citing the need for extra makeup to compensate for the bright lights, Ny wielded her brushes until we could barely recognize ourselves and each other.

In fact, our close friend Sam Vassel later confessed that he didn't recognize us either till after we began to sing. He joked that he had then renamed us Sights and Sounds Incorporated. But we felt pretty and sophisticated. We had rehearsed and we had prayed. That would do.

So as the curtains opened and my eyes adjusted enough to take in the crowd, I was crushed and at once so very thankful that our shared stage fright had caused us girls to be gripping the hand of the person next to us.

Poor Janet! She became my lifeline, as I drowned in despair. Somehow the lyrics to the songs fought their way to the surface amid the myriad of thoughts that pinballed inside my brain.

"How could he?!"

"And couldn't he have chosen another seat?"

"Yes, she was nice... and pretty too."

"Look what's become of us!"

"GOD, did YOU really speak to me at all?"

Somehow, I managed to make it through the first half. As soon as the curtain closed, I beat a hasty retreat to the seclusion of the backstage area and hid in a corner to be alone with my thoughts. Or at least that was my plan.

As my friend Janet was used to reminding me, "Man ah plan, an' GOD ah wipe out." For as surely as I was seated there, HIS voice pierced through my anguished thoughts. I was not alone.

"Why are you upset?"

"Let him check out other girls."

"That's how he will realize they are not you, and that you are what he really needs."

If there ever was a halftime Pep Talk, that was it. I returned to the stage rejuvenated and re-energized. I didn't need to hear a rallying cry like the one, Nerissa, the girl who would become our lead soprano would sweetly chirp: "Bounce on stage, girls!" I was ready for this. Fixed on my well-painted lips was a huge smile. I was in on the game plan. I was getting a glimpse of how GOD thought, and I liked HIS mind.

So isn't it ironic that the first "date" we have as a newly minted couple is at one of our concerts? This time he sat unaccompanied staring dreamy-eyed at me on the stage. GOD does have a sense of humor. I was in seventh heaven all weekend.

That Monday morning, Selwyn was again under the tree in the center of the Arts Faculty. This was no accident. He did not hide the fact that he had been waiting to see me. As I quickened my step to join him, I could sense an apprehension in his gaze. Something was amiss.

Selwyn drew me aside and, apologizing profusely, declared that he was still having doubts about us. His interval of considering other girls for the position of wife had left him confused. He was no longer sure I was the one. That was a tremendous blow.

Shockingly, however, I found that I was reassuring him.

I was telling him not to stress over it.

That GOD would reveal the right one for him.

That I would help him pray.

That what I wanted was GOD's best for him.

That I never ever wanted him to feel pressure from me. The most bizarre part of this whole situation was that I believed every word I was saying.

That had to be GOD. It was a very strange dichotomy. On the one hand, I knew how I felt and that I wanted him. On the other hand, I felt that it was GOD who had made me a promise, not Selwyn, so it was up to GOD to fulfill HIS word without pressure from me.

Not much else changed in our relationship. I continued to send the notes and to pray as GOD led me. By then this was a habit I had embraced, and I became quite comfortable with being the conduit of GOD's love to Selwyn with no strings attached.

Then one day it happened. GOD told me to stop—stop sending notes,

stop calling,

just stop.

It may be hard to imagine that the girl who had been so adamant about the proper protocol of a boy-girl relation-ship now found it hard to stop telling a boy who was uncertain of his feelings that she loved him. But there I was. I knew the next move had to be his.

17

You're Going to Do What?

Earlier I mentioned my friend in our band who so faithfully helped me stay obedient to the word of the LORD. What I didn't do was fill you in on his story, so here goes.

Remember how I had been praying that the LORD would honor his faithfulness? Well the LORD did do just that! A few months after I had begun to pray this prayer, I stumbled upon an unusual scene.

It was a Sunday evening, and if my memory serves me well, our group, New Creation, had ministered at a concert close to the home of our mentor, Raphael Mason. His home had become a regular hangout for our group, so it was natural that we gravitated to it when we were in the vicinity. And that's how I walked in on a peculiar scene.

Two of our members, one of them being my dear friend for whom I had been praying, were sitting opposite each other with a deer-in-the headlights expression pasted on their faces. The air was charged with a sense that something momentous had taken place between them.

When they could finally respond to my greeting, and my question of what was going on, it was in a voice just above a whisper. They said they were going to marry each other.

Now it was my turn to have the wide-eyed expression. Add to that a fully slack-jawed open mouth. What were they talking about? These guys could barely stand each other!

Yes, we all loved each other as a group. And yes, we generally got on very well together. But these two were always at loggerheads. Maybe that was because my dear friend, the piano player, was wont to be exceedingly annoying, and she, the lead singer, was known to be just a tad bit high strung. Not a match I, or anyone else in the group for that matter, would have ever considered.

But there they were staring doe-eyed at each other, (I know that's the common phrase, but, seriously, have you ever looked into the soulful eyes of a donkey?) They were at once excited and scared. And there was this Presence that made me know this was not a joke. This was serious. To cut a long story short, pretty soon Al and Marjorie were an engaged couple about to plan a wedding.

18

On Bended Knee

It was the 1982 Easter holidays and Selwyn, who had again become aloof, disappeared to his junior-doctor brother's cottage at the Princess Margaret hospital in the rural parish of St Thomas. It was clear that he was in turmoil and had gone there to clear his head.

By this time, Marjorie and Al were solidly a couple and frequent visitors to the townhouse I shared with a childhood neighbor and family friend. She, a middle-aged single woman, had offered for me to stay at her Liguanea home while I completed my final year of university.

Our family had moved from our convenient university housing in College Commons, because my mother needed to resign from her teaching position with the university, in order to pursue doctoral studies in the USA.

With that, my final year saw me happily sharing space with Rachel McLean who also welcomed my stream of friends. And that is how that night Al said his goodbyes from her home, and left Marjorie and me to our sleepover.

We lived in a townhouse. For those who don't understand the concept, let me explain, because this knowledge will prove useful if you want to understand what comes next. A townhouse is a row of joined houses. In our case it was a row of two-story houses, and we were the second to last at the end of the row. Hold on to that detail. It will explain why I responded to Marjorie with the bemused patience of a mother trying to soothe her groggy child back to bed after an episode of bizarre "sleep talk."

I had gotten up in time to hear Miss McLean, as we called her, shut the door and leave for work. As all serious UWI students know, the Easter holidays were a crucial time of preparation for the upcoming final exams. That's why I'm going to imagine we had spent some part of the night in serious study and were, therefore, finding it difficult to start the day. It may or may not have happened that way.

I do know, however, that it had to be at least 7:30 a.m. I had just re-entered the bedroom from the adjoining bathroom, when Marjorie bolted out of bed, walked over to the rear-facing window of my second-floor bedroom and, peering through the louvers at the backyard, declared that Selwyn was outside.

Now, remember the detail I asked you to hold on to? That one about the configuration of a townhouse? Yes, that one. Well, here is where this detail comes in handy.

Selwyn couldn't have possibly been in our backyard. He was all the way in St Thomas. And even if he had returned to Kingston, there was no way for him to be in our backyard. One's only access to one's backyard in a townhouse is from having first passed through one's own front door. Marjorie had to be mistaken. She must have been sleep talking.

With that in mind, and in the spirit of humoring rather than antagonizing a sleepwalker, I sidled over to the window and in my most placating tone I said, "See Marjorie, Selwyn is not..."

I stopped in mid-sentence; the words trapped in my throat. For as I peered through the louvers, I found myself staring into the grinning, upturned face of none other than Selwyn Lloyd Batchelor. How was that possible?!

Miss McLean had already left for work. She had securely locked the doors and security gates. How did he gain access to our backyard?! For him to do that, he would have had to scale a few fences and walk through the back-yards of nearly all our neighbors along the row!

But there he was in the flesh! My "sleep-walker" friend, Marjorie had actually responded to the sound of pebbles hitting against the window louvers. My rear-facing bed-room paired with Miss McLean's having already left for work, made it impossible for anyone to hear Selwyn's re-peated knocks at the outer front gate.

Undaunted and determined, he had done the unthink-able. He had trespassed through a row of at least six backyards before finally arriving below my bedroom win-dow.

Cue the panic. I had not long got out of bed. I hadn't even yet washed my face or brushed my teeth. I was still in my pajamas. How was I going to get myself looking presentable enough to let him in?!

"Good fren betta dan pocket money." That's the Jamai-can proverb that took on new meaning at that point. Marjorie would keep him distracted at the window, while I did the super shuffle of a speed change. I may have missed a few steps in my ablutions, but heart racing and palms sweaty, I managed to open the back door, and then the grilled gate, all the while painfully aware that my every move was under scrutiny. He hadn't taken his eyes off me.

Sensing the moment, Marj, who had been unceremoniously awakened from her sleep and had herself not had time to properly dress, let alone have breakfast, hurriedly stashed her things into her overnight bag and made a hasty exit.

In an instant, I was alone with the man who I now claimed as the love of my life. But nothing prepared me for what happened next.

I cannot tell you what my eyes were doing before they caught sight of the sudden movement that brought Selwyn to his knees in front of me. Wide-eyed and unprepared for this, I sat in shock as he again offered a heartfelt apology for his aloofness and his admittedly hasty retreat to the beach town of Lyssons, St Thomas where his brother lived.

He confessed that he had come to realize that he had been searching for me among all the other girls who had held his interest. He had now settled it in his heart that I was in truth the only one he wanted. Remember what GOD had told me at the Ward Theatre concert?

I can't say that amid the swirl that was my brain I heard most of what he had to say. What I've been left with are strobe-like flashes of memory.

Him on his knees.

His hand outstretched.

The small King Conch shell it contained.

His head on my lap,

and finally, his mouth on mine.

What was happening? And so very quickly!

Many kisses were exchanged that day in between the rush of words, as we tried to make up for all our lost times of closeness. He explained how he had, like Jonah, run to the sea and there had found a jewel sparkling at the bottom of the ocean. He had dived to retrieve and clean up what I now held in my hand. It was his gift to me—this jewel of the sea which he had presented on his knees.

19

The Date

Remember my friends in the band, Al and Marjorie, who became an instant couple? Here is where our stories collide.

I remember the day like it was yesterday, Al and Marjorie had taken the day off from lectures (yes, in the midst of all the goings-on, we were all still university students) and had each gone their separate way within the University's Chapel Gardens to seek the LORD regarding the exact date on which they should marry.

I remember Marjorie coming to let me know in an awed voice that GOD had given them both, *separately*, the exact wedding date!

After we talked, I recall myself staring through the bars of the window of H4, Mary Seacole Hall. What I said next would forever change my life.

Without so much as a "Dear Heavenly FATHER or any such holy preamble, I turned to the LORD, and I said, "Well if YOU can tell them when they should get married, YOU can tell me too." That was it.

That was my presumptuous prayer. I truthfully did not expect an answer. But just as quickly as I had said it, so instantaneous was the response, "December 28." That was it. Alone in the room, I ran to the calendar near the room door, and flipping hastily through its pages, I made a discovery that made me doubt GOD had spoken after all.

The year was 1982. That year December 28 fell on a Tuesday. There were some days in the week that were traditionally reserved for weddings. Those were Saturday, Sunday, and even Wednesday. But never in my life had I heard of a bride getting married in a proper wedding ceremony on a Tuesday. And to add to the incredulity of the situation, it was a long-held desire of mine to have a morning wedding. It would be unlikely for someone to get time off from work for a Tuesday morning wedding. So no, I naively thought. GOD could not have spoken. For of course, HE would need to be bound by the traditions of men. Looking back, I now wonder if GOD ever rolls HIS eyes.

This was my conclusion: I had spoken frivolously, and my frivolous mind had concocted a frivolous date. Nevertheless, I decided to write it down just in case...

So, now you know what I said—the question that changed my life. For you see, even though my words were flippantly spoken, and the answer seemed absurd, I couldn't shake the feeling that maybe, just maybe, GOD had indeed spoken.

With that came a returned resolve to have things revert to the usual and customary protocol. GOD would tell him the date. He would propose. I would accept, and we would get married and live happily ever after. Finally, a chance to regain some self-respect.

Of course, by now you know that this is not how things went. Right? A pattern was emerging. GOD was continuing to stand outside of any box I had carefully and even prettily made for HIM. Shockingly, HE had other plans that didn't really need any input from me!

As we raced through the chaos of young love and final exams in June, I impatiently began to badger GOD. "Surely YOU don't expect me to also tell him the date?!" By then, I was in my final year of university. The year was 1982. The date GOD had given me was December 28, 1982. Now you see why I was beginning to be impatient?

20

Fishers of Men

Now, I'm noticing some patterns. January 28, 1982, was when the LORD began to bring HIS word to pass before my eyes. The date HE gave me as our wedding day was December 28 of the same year. What I failed to let you know was of another really important series of events that took place just before that year began.

I started this journey of recollection by referencing my parents. Here is where some of their own love story intersects with mine. My mom had left Jamaica to pursue her PhD in the USA. She would return for a few milestone events, and one of them was her wedding anniversary in November of 1981. For this occasion, made even more special by months of separation, my dad had presented her with a new set of rings to replace the band he had given her on their wedding day, 23 years before. As soon as she received this gift, she in turn surprised me by giving me her old wedding band. What a moment!

I still recall our fascination with our mother's fingers, and the way we would twist and work the wedding band, until we could slip it from her ring finger. I remember examining its facets and trying it on my tiny finger before returning it to hers.

Now it was mine. I could keep it forever, and wear it on my own hand! The hand I chose was my right hand. And it still fit loosely on my ring finger, which I chose as the carrier of the precious cargo. I was very careful to reserve the ring finger of my left hand for my own special band.

But what does that have to do with my story of love you ask? Patience! All will be revealed in time.

It was the last day of December 1981, New Year's Eve. Our band had been asked to minister at an event put on in May Pen by a community group called Fishers of Men. It was a lovely evening marked by the fellowship of believers and the presence of our LORD.

Before long, it was nearing midnight. The organizers began the countdown to ring in the New Year. I was by then standing at the back of the hall taking in the festivities. Suddenly, as the old year was changing to the new, I was aware of HIS voice. "Take the ring from your right hand and place it on your left hand, for by next year this time, you will be married." What?! I wasn't even in a relationship at that point! Was I going crazy?

By then I knew enough to recognize the voice of the LORD when I heard it, so glancing furtively around to make sure no one was watching, I slipped the ring from my right hand and deposited it loosely onto my left ring finger.

I felt like such a fool. And let's not mention self-conscious. It seemed like there was a spotlight on me in this dimly lit room, and everyone was gaping at me pretending to be married. Just as I feared, I was soon called out.

I had composed myself just enough to join my band near the front of the hall, when it happened. It was Keith, our drummer. He took one look at me and said, "Is when since you married, mi dear?!" For those who know Keith, you know he usually speaks in a volume just loud enough to be audible. But at that moment, to my ears, he seemed to be trumpeting my embarrassment for all to hear. That was it.

I quickly slipped the offending circle from the ring finger and transferred it to my middle finger. I then bargained with the LORD to consider I was being obedient by keeping it as close as possible to the intended destination. Given that it was also likely to be lost from that finger, since it was more slender, I believe I got HIS approval. So, all of 1982, I wore the ring there and remembered HIS promise.

21

Thursday Girl

I mentioned that I had confided my deepest desires to my Best Friend. Well, embedded in my three-part plan, was another desire. Before marriage, I wanted to experience the freedom and excitement of sharing an apartment with close friends. By a pretty serendipitous turn of events, I got my wish. It came through a feisty, jocular, erudite Ghanaian-Jamaican girl with the traditional Ghanaian name, Aba. It simply meant she was a girl born on a Thursday. But "simple" was not a word that could describe my Aba. Unless of course, it was something like "simply wonderful!"

Aba saw me. That's what I remember most about her. She could always remind me who I was. My memory of our first meeting was orientation at UWI in 1979.

"No", Aba corrected me, "I first saw you when both our high school Spanish classes met at the Caenwood Centre, when you were in 6th form." And of course, she was right. I just didn't see her.

Always with a welcoming smile and that playful twinkle in her eye, she greeted me at our orientation at the University of the West Indies, and later when we again met at the IVCF. It was then that she began her role as my UWI mother.

We were pursuing the same major, and had all our classes together. How blessed I was to have this good fortune! I still tell my children about this and unashamedly credit Aba with the fact that I, this scatter-brained student, ended up with an honors degree from UWI.

Plainly stated, Aba was my guide throughout my UWI career. I cannot count the number of notes (there were no cell phones) I received from Aba reminding me of what assignments I had and when they were due.

Aba arrived at UWI with her best friend Faith, also known as Betty. They recount that they used to refer to me as DT in the notes they frequently passed to each other (they were the original text "messagers").

Recently Aba reminded me that it was while Betty was away from university for a bit that she chose to spend more time with me. It was Aba who graciously drew me into their circle, when Betty returned, and began calling me DT to my face. That name has stuck with me through the years.

In short order, we became a triumvirate cementing ourselves in some people's minds as Betty, Aba and Diane— B.A.D, the singing group. This came about simply because we never stopped harmonizing all the way from Kingston to St Elizabeth (a four-hour ride), as we rode the bus together through the rolling countryside to our first IVCF Christmas Camp at Oceanview, Lovers Leap, in the breadbasket parish of St Elizabeth. (Stories from that camp could be another book in itself.)

Even though journalist Ian Boyne in his *Gleaner* article later labeled our singing as "not so melodious," we could frequently be heard in the bathroom of the Creative Arts Centre, which we chose for its awesome acoustics, reminding anyone in earshot of our singing, that "You need a song in your heart at night."

Aba was also one of my prayer partners during my time of turmoil in accepting the wait. I still remember the day we ended a round of prayer and fasting in the Chapel Gardens. We left with a deep sense of calm. A great spiritual battle had been won, and I only had to wait to see what GOD would do. I had Aba to thank for walking with me and holding up my hand during that fight. I remain ever thankful for her prayers.

Apparently, my friend Aba's mothering overflowed even to my life after campus. Neither of us recalls this, but I have the recently found note to prove that it was Aba who had made the appointment for my job interview at Immaculate Conception High (ICHS) right after our leaving UWI.

It was my first job, and I had the joy of being her work colleague in the Spanish Department as well as being her Homeroom neighbor. I was delighted to be able to share in her passion for the girls, as we hosted retreats at the Aquinas Centre. We shared our lives and love for the LORD with eager young women.

It was in these settings that Aba was in her element. She mothered us all, commandeering the kitchen and drawing us all into a deeper seeking of the LORD.

22

The Apartment

How lovely it was that GOD granted my desire to share an apartment with friends before I got married, by once again having Aba see me. She must have realized how miserable I was becoming with my new living arrangement, for at her invitation I got to share an apartment with her and her sister Adjoa.

I vividly recall the wave of relief that washed over me when I received the message that our former Linguistics professor, Dr. Christie, would be travelling for a while and needed someone to house-sit her beautiful Constant Spring Road apartment. I had been offered the job at Immaculate Conception High School (ICHS), and since our family home was some distance away in Spanish Town, that made it necessary for me to move to the city.

I had rented a room in a townhouse close enough to the school. In no time, however, I began to be uncomfortable with sharing space with a total stranger. Aba's invitation to join them in the apartment was more than welcome! The apartment, replete with elevator and a swimming pool (a novelty at the time), made us feel like we were moving into the lap of luxury. For me, leaving an address farther down the road to one higher up on Constant Spring Road, this was literally "moving on up to a deluxe apartment in the sky-yi-yi!"

The lovely apartment became the scene of some of my greatest battles with the LORD. It was there, in late 1982, that I hit a crisis of faith. I had earlier told the LORD that the latest sensible time for Selwyn to propose would be August. I recall how the LORD had literally made this chocolate-colored woman blush in shame, when HE reminded me that HIS ways, and thoughts were infinitely superior to mine. Truthfully, till then, I really believed only paler-colored folk could blush. But that summer day, as I lay in bed questioning the LORD, the words of Isaiah 55:8-11, took on a power and forcefulness that made my cheeks glow red-hot.

'For My thoughts are not your thoughts, Nor are your ways My ways,' declares the LORD. 'For as the heavens are higher than the earth, So are My ways higher than your ways And My thoughts higher than your thoughts. For as the rain and snow come down from heaven, And do not return there without watering the earth, Making it bear and sprout, And providing seed to the sower and bread to the eater, So will My word be which goes out of My mouth; It will not return to Me void (useless, without result), Without accomplishing what I desire, And without succeeding in the matter for which I sent it' (Isaiah 55:8-11, AMP).

I wonder if HE then dropped the mic?

23

The End of My Rope

Y ou would think after that, I was settled in my wait. After all, hadn't GOD proven HIMSELF enough so far? Wasn't I by then convinced that HIS plans were better than mine? The short answer? No.

I maintained that if we were to get married when HE said, I should not have been still waiting for a proposal in September. I became anxious enough that I finally convinced myself that despite my begging HIM not to allow me to be deceived, GOD had allowed me to listen to and follow the voice of the Enemy after all. How could HE?

I was done. Done listening to HIM. Done talking to HIM. Especially after I had made the desperate, expensive phone call to my mother in Pennsylvania asking her to help me pray for clarity and direction, and she had called back some weeks later to say, the LORD wasn't leading her to pray about it! Seriously!! HE wasn't leading her to pray about it!! HE was being mean. I was so done.

You have to imagine that Selwyn, who by then was finishing up his final year on campus and teaching Science at a boys' high school, was a frequent visitor to our apartment. After all, we were still in a relationship.

Having been assured that it was not for me to divulge the date on which we should get married, I watched him askance during our times together to see if he was ever going to propose. I'll let you out of your misery. The answer was no.

It was one day, possibly in November or early December, that without thinking, I bowed my head and thanked GOD for the meal I was about to eat. As clearly as one can hear the voice of GOD inaudibly, HE said to me, "So you're speaking to ME."

Like a fog before wind, my resentment dissipated. My heart softened and I admitted my desperate need for HIM in my life. Peter's words in John 6:68 became my deep cry.

"LORD, to whom shall I go? YOU alone have the words of eternal life. YOU are my only hope." But there was an addendum. "No more speaking to me, please. I'm confused enough as it is."

24

A December Wedding

Nevertheless, as I watched the days of December pass by, I begged HIM to please let Selwyn propose.

Somehow, during our many hours of conversation, Selwyn had surmised that I had a wedding date I believed the LORD had given to me. I was very careful not to reveal the details to him. So, I suffered in silence when December brought us the wedding of yet another of our band members.

The year 1982 had seen the joining in holy matrimony of Marjorie and Al in June, Vangie and Keith in July, and, a bit unexpectedly, by mid-year Janet and Chris were planning a December 19 wedding. It was then that I came to a decision.

I would remain in the relationship till December 28. If that date passed, and we were still not husband and wife, it would mark the end of our relationship. For surely, if all this was not of the LORD, I was most certainly ensnared in a horrible web of deception orchestrated by the Enemy of my soul.

I would also be terribly embarrassed, as, led by what I had thought was the voice of the LORD, I had shared the date with a few singled-out people. My life and reputation were on the brink of utter ruin.

Unfortunately for Janet, my face in her wedding photos betrayed my abject disconsolation. I could hardly fake my signature smile. I dreaded the coming days.

A very upbeat and unusually chatty Selwyn was my date at the wedding. That evening, after he accompanied me back to the empty apartment, he was also unusually amorous. He always was. But this was heightened.

So heightened that he had me change out of my sack-like housedress to put on something he would consider less sexy. When I complied and returned in a dress that went way past my knee, he responded that this was even worse.

That was when I began to inwardly give him the stink eye. He was obviously being used by the Devil trying to trap me into sexual sin. That was the plan! I was not ignorant of his devices.

Inwardly I dared him to let Selwyn put a hand on me. I was ready. My foreboding and Selwyn's lighthearted chatter were interrupted by a knock on our door. It was the newly married couple. True to the sisterly nature of our friendship, Janet had stopped by to pick up my favorite blue dress to add to her honeymoon "couture."

25

Chitty Chitty Bang Bang

As I closed the door and returned to *Chitty Chitty Bang Bang*, the movie we were watching amid Selwyn's chatter, he said something that caused my heart to lurch.

"I feel like I should be going on my honeymoon now."

It was a monologue received with an icy stare.

"Yes, I remember when the LORD told me to get married in December."

Ice turned to fire. What did he just say? The LORD told him to get married in December?!

My stomach filled up with a thousand butterflies. My heart was pounding mercilessly. I could hardly hear the rest of what he had to say.

I was now ready to join the conversation. Ready to pour out all I had been keeping pent up inside.

Firmly GOD's voice broke through the chaos that was my mind. "Don't tell him the date."

I reengaged in time to hear Selwyn continue.

"In August while I was doing my summer job in the swamp, I thought the LORD told me to get married this December. But I told HIM not this December. Maybe next December, or at the earliest next year August."

At this my heart nearly burst. I had asked the LORD to tell Selwyn to propose in August! The LORD had in fact spoken to him!!

I was beside myself. My faithful LORD, my Best Friend had not been leading me along! It was Selwyn's nonchalance that had caused all this reason for doubt.

To say I was relieved was a massive understatement. I had not been deceived after all! My thanks to GOD knew no bounds.

Of course, one undeniable fact stared me in the face. This was December 19. The date I had been given was December 28, a mere nine days away. A wedding on that date was impossible, so I could at least unburden myself and tell him of my yearlong trauma. But again, came the firm command.

"Do not tell him the date!"

While I was internally arguing with the LORD, I caught sight of Selwyn out of his seat on the sofa and pacing the floor animatedly. What was going on?!

With a strange expression, at once excited and serene, he asked to see a calendar. Now here is where I will need to remind you of a few things, as well as fill you in on a few other details:

My father is a no-nonsense man.

I am the first daughter in my Jamaican family (translated this means big wedding).

My father is a no-nonsense man.

Back to our evening.

26

The Calendar

Selwyn is pacing. He asks to see a calendar. Scanning the apartment, I quickly ascertain that the only calendar in our shared space is in the room that my friend Aba and her sister Adjoa share.

This Sunday evening, they have both gone home to spend time with the rest of their family. They won't mind the intrusion. I direct Selwyn to the calendar on the wall in their bedroom. I remain standing in the living room. I am numb.

Remember I told you that December 28, 1982 fell on a Tuesday? Bear that in mind, as you join me standing alone in the living room while Selwyn scrutinizes the calendar in my friends' bedroom.

Feel with me the exultancy that I have in truth been led by my loving LORD. This is paired with the terrible dread, resignation even, that there was no way Selwyn would choose the date I had been given.

Then feel with me, as he emerges from their room, an almost unearthly calm surrounding him.

"Diane", he says in a voice thick with holy fear.

"If the date I have in my mind, coincides with the date you believe the LORD told you, I will have to speak with your father."

He then looks me directly in the eye and says, "December 28."

Now try to put an emotional flood the size of the Congo's 11-million-gallon-a-second waterfall, Inga, into words. I can't either, so I won't try.

Oh, you're wondering about that obscure waterfall? Well, let's just say Niagara Falls is only the 11th largest waterfall in the world. The wonders of marketing! But back to my apartment living room.

I am simultaneously laughing and crying. My GOD did speak!

HIS voice was real!

HE had guided and directed me after all!

I could die of sheer joy.

When Selwyn can again speak, he tells how the number 28 came into his mind. He recounts how on seeing where it fell on the calendar, he battled with the day. How he mentally suggested the Saturday or the Sunday, as he was sure those were the more likely days I would have chosen. How the number 28 stubbornly seemed to spiral beginning like a little dot from the recesses of his mind, growing big and bold then taking center stage. He had no choice but to say the date he had been given.

So, have you been holding your breath this whole time? Breathe. Relax. Settle yourself while I continue my story.

I rushed to my bedroom to grab my notebook with the wedding guest list I had compiled months before, gears rapidly shifting into planning mode. I was for sure now going to marry Selwyn Lloyd Batchelor on December 28, 1982 come hell or high water (as my mother would say).

But there was one hitch. Selwyn insisted that if this was from the LORD, my father would have to agree. So, let's review those points again:

My father is a no-nonsense man.

I am the first daughter in my Jamaican family (translated this means big wedding).

My father is a no-nonsense man.

I failed to mention that while watching *Chitty Chitty Bang Bang*, we had been engaged in wrapping presents to take home for the Christmas holidays. This was our first Christmas of being real working adults with a salary. We were excited to share the meager but nonetheless gratifying fruit of our teaching labor with our families.

The next day would see us headed to Spanish Town. Before separating for the night, we agreed to meet at my home the next day, when Selwyn would ask my father for my hand in marriage.

And in case you missed it, you just witnessed the closest thing to a proposal I ever had. Missed it? Back up a bit. Here's a hint. It begins with "If the date..." Now you know why I still treasure the memory of the bended knee and the conch shell. But seriously, (and cornily, I know) I have to admit that I treasure the giver so much more than that gift.

27

Yes Now, Spanish Town!

True to his word, Selwyn arrived at my Ensom City home at about 2 p.m. the next day. Ensom City, a growing middle-class community of bungalows in the suburbs of the seventeenth century city Spanish Town, was where our family called home. It was in Spanish Town that Selwyn and I had met at St Jago High School, and where my mother had taught before becoming a lecturer at the University of the West Indies.

My mother had returned to the island from her doctoral studies in the U.S.A. to spend the Christmas holidays with us. My sister and my two brothers who were still living at home were all there. My older brother, Donny, had married his childhood sweetheart Louella the year before, so he was in his own home in the parish of Portland.

Since Selwyn was no stranger to our family, he mingled easily, engaging in chitchat while I eyed him quizzically and expectantly. When was he going to approach my father? The suspense was unbearable. I suffered through the dinner which he was eventually invited to share with us, and sat in stony silence, as the hours chimed from our living room clock.

I consoled myself with the fact that marriage to Selwyn was really an aside. The main event had already taken place. I had indisputable proof that my LORD, my First Love, was alive and active in my life and that HE did not trifle with my emotions. That right there was gold! I didn't need a man's ring to assure me I was deeply loved.

With that, somewhere close to 10 p.m., after my parents had both retired for the night, I approached Selwyn to suggest that maybe he needed to go home now. My gentle tone belied my true impulse, which was to shout, "Gwaan a yu yaad!" (Go home! Add the strong emotion.) Selwyn had other plans. He admitted that he was scared, but that he was determined and ready to speak to my father.

So, here's some more useful information. Our father had completely carpeted our four-bedroom, two-bathroom, reinforced concrete bungalow. I said completely, because I do want you to understand that even the kitchen and bathrooms in our tropical home were carpeted. Why is this important to know you ask? Well, here's why.

When I tiptoed through the open door of my parents' pitch-black bedroom to check if they were awake, no one should have heard me. In truth, I had only done it to humor Selwyn. So, imagine my shock when, as I was retreating, I heard my father's voice arising from the darkness.

"What is it?", he queried. I stopped in my tracks, spun around and found enough voice to let him know that Selwyn wished to speak with him. "Let him come in," he responded.

Seriously! He was allowing Selwyn into their bedroom! And at this hour, while they were already in bed! Befuddled, I relayed the invitation to Selwyn and led him to their, by then, lamp-lit bedroom.

Again, I will not pretend to recall the exact sequence of events. I'll only attempt to share what my baffled brain could retain. Surreal dreamscape. That's how the scene progressed:

Selwyn's blurting out "Mr. Thompson, I believe the LORD told Diane and I to get married next week Tuesday."

My father's eyes shooting up to the ceiling.

Selwyn's running headlong into his story of how the LORD had been working in his life over the past year and ending with asking my father's blessing to marry me.

I was a bystander watching it all unfold. A fly on the wall even.

The next person to speak was my mother. Remember she was privy to my dilemma when I had called her in Pennsylvania to ask for her help in praying for guidance on this very matter? This was not as much of a shock to her. I cannot now recall her exact words, but it was something more on the encouraging side. This trend was abruptly cut short when my dad burst out,

"What am I going to tell my family?" (and he had a lot).

"What am I going to tell my friends?" (and he had a lot of those too).

As a matter of fact, I had the opportunity to see the friends and family dynamic in full play at Donny's wedding the year before. Having myself needed a few full days to recover from the stress of being involved, I had again reiterated my desire to have a small, no-frills wedding.

In truth, I had taken it even further. In order to avoid stress altogether, my proposal was for my groom and I to dress up, get married privately, get good photos, then send a photo and a portion of boxed wedding cake to all our loved ones. An impossible dream! But a girl could dream.

I resigned myself to my father continuing along the vein in which he had begun. But, after those two lines, what he said next was totally unexpected. "But..." He began with the word "but." This is how he continued:

"But, if you believe this is what the LORD is saying to you, I will give you my blessing and put $10,000 towards your wedding plans." (That was when our Jamaican currency still had some value).

With that he got out of bed, prayed a prayer of blessing and handed me over to Selwyn. Just like that. The impossible had become my reality.

Before I could take it in, I found myself being asked if I wished to join my father in driving Selwyn home. Just for context, you need to know that by then it was midnight. You also need to be aware that Selwyn had left my home on quite a few occasions prior to this at a very late hour. Never once before had my father offered him a ride home.

I was in a daze. What I think I remember is that on the ride back home, my dad took the opportunity to prepare me for a wedding without friends and family. I was prepared.

I was not prepared, however, for the wide-eyed sleepless night I spent after waking my sister to inform her that I was getting married the next Tuesday. I don't know if it was sleep-induced, but she pretty calmly congratulated me and went right back to sleep leaving me alone with the strangest emotion.

I felt abandoned. There. I said it. I couldn't believe how easily my dad had handed me over to a strange man! I can imagine GOD must have been sniggering. Wasn't this the miracle for which I had prayed during the mean time?

When daylight came, I informed the rest of the family. The same calm response greeted me. (Well my pragmatic, law-student brother Bruce had a few things to add, but that's his way). Even my baby brother Dexter, then a student at the high school where Selwyn taught, just casually accepted it. It was almost as if they had all been expecting it.

That morning Daddy again invited me into their bedroom. This time it was to ask if, maybe, I would consider getting engaged on December 28 and then get married

sometime in January. Emboldened by how things had progressed, I countered that, if GOD had worked so far to fulfill
HIS word, I would be obedient and get married on the date
HE had told me. At this point my dad proceeded to give me
a strong reality check:

> I would not be able to get married in a church at such
> short notice.
>
> I would not have friends or family celebrate with me
> (It was a major holiday period, most of my friends
> were already away from the city on vacation).
>
> I would not have wedding gifts.
>
> I would not have a honeymoon.

Undeterred, I countered that we were prepared to face
those possibilities. With that, he was again on board
offering to help me in whatever way he could.

The Dress

So I mentioned the fact that my brother had married the Caymanian-Jamaican beauty, Louella, in June of the previous year. What I didn't say was how this impacted my present reality.

You see, Louella and I were uncannily alike. We were both five feet one and a half inches tall. We both weighed less than a hundred pounds, and we both wore size six shoes. This fact was to play a very important part in my hurry-come-up (speedy) wedding plans. When Louella's mail-ordered wedding dress arrived on the island, she opened the package and displayed the dress for me to see.

It was very beautiful, but not the style I had in mind for my own wedding. In fact, I had already been carrying around a sketch of a ballerina style ball gown with a cinched waistline, which I had planned to pair with satin ballerina shoes.

Of course, I couldn't bring myself to tell that to Louella, when she declared that, after she wore her dream dress, it was to be mine. I would wait for the euphoria of her wedding to be over, and then I would break it to her gently.

Well, that didn't happen. Louella changed out of her wedding dress in my bedroom and left me the dress and veil lying on my bed. With that, she was off on her honeymoon. So, in order to use my bed again, I was forced to store a used wedding dress in my closet.

And that was how the 20th of December 1982, found me handing over a soiled wedding dress to a stunned but willing accomplice, my dear friend Marjorie. On hearing the news, she had offered to carefully hand wash the used dress and have it ready for my big day.

To complete the ensemble, I dispatched a message to my sister-in-law Louella, who then lived in the countryside of Portland, to please bring the underskirt and shoes in time for me to wear them to the wedding. And that's exactly what she did.

29

Nine-Day Wonder

If you're Jamaican, the title sets it up. If you're not, let me help you. That's the phrase we give to something usually pretty amazing that happens seemingly overnight.

It would take a great many words to regale you with the details of all that led up to the wedding:

The meetings between our family and Selwyn's. (They thought their methodical son had surely lost his mind).

The rejected request made to Selwyn's family church (The request was made only to placate the family's already raw nerves, as our dream venue had always been the UWI chapel. Since the church had not done the mandatory marriage counseling, they declined to participate in the wedding).

The phone call to Raphael Mason, our Covenant Group (small/care group) leader, who also happened to be a marriage officer, to ask whether he would be prepared to officiate at the wedding. He said he would.

The phone call Raphael in turn made to our pastor, Peter Morgan, who summarily demanded we come to see him, as this was clearly an ill-conceived, hare-brained scheme. He would need to straighten out "these crazy kids" and restore us to our right minds.

The right about turn that followed our meeting with Peter Morgan. "I'll do anything I can to help you." His willingness to co-officiate at the wedding. His driving us around for hours in search of a home where we could live together after our wedding.

The deferred acquisition of my custom wedding band. (It was the maddening Christmas rush. The best they could do was size the gold band I was already wearing on my middle finger, so it would fit my ring finger. And that's what we did.)

112

The impossible acquisition of the coveted University Chapel as the wedding venue.

The wedding invitations on fancy stationery that my friend Aba had her then boyfriend, now husband, Bruce, handwrite for quick distribution.

The "chance" rendezvous with so many of our friends, who quickly spread the word like a wildfire about our "hurry-come-up" wedding. (I still remember my dear friend Dulcie Linton's amused quip when she got in earshot of me on the wedding day. "You first me!" she chuckled. Translated, I had beaten her in a race. Dulcie and Andrew had been planning their wedding many months in advance, and were next in the line of our circle of friends who were engaged to be married).

New Creation's all-hands-on-deck response, so much so that apart from handing over my skeleton wish list of a wedding program, I had nothing more to do with its execution. I still recall Cleve's admonition to "Just relax. Everything is under control" and Cheryl's mad dash to the chapel door to hand me the bouquet of roses and Euphorbia Marginata

(Jamaican Christmas flowers) while apologizing that the flower shop had no Queen Anne's Lace. That was a happy accident. Every Christmas in Jamaica when these green bushes inexplicably turn white, I'm reminded of my very own Christmas miracle.

The very relaxed Christmas day spent with my family—my very last as Diane Thompson. Well, not exactly. I became a Thompson again many years later. I hope curiosity makes you stick around to hear that story.

Ok, Ok, you caught me. You know I'm not good at glossing over the details. I have to put just a little more meat on these bones. So here goes:

Selwyn, fully on board with the wedding plans, began to reveal the many ways GOD had been leading him during all those months of silence. He was certain we were to be married at the University Chapel. He was certain, he said, because months before he had had a vision of me in a wedding veil. What stood out to him from the surroundings in the vision was the chapel's distinctive railing at the altar. With that, my dad offered to drive us to the university to see if our miracle would extend to being able to have our wedding in that most sought-after venue.

With lively Christmas music as our soundtrack and my dad's fingers drumming happily on the steering wheel, we were off to a promising start. On our thirty-minute drive from Spanish Town into Kingston, the already glorious December weather took on an extra-special glow. Cooled by Christmas breezes, under sparkling azure skies, the Mandela Highway seemed to zip open the lush, sun-dappled cane fields that flanked it. The majestic hills which formed the backdrop against which our island city shone, looked even more beautiful in their tones of deep blues and verdant greens dotted with the happy colors of ever-multiplying homes.

As we drew nearer to our destination, the beautiful campus came into view. In fact, the approach to the University of the West Indies was framed by the impressive Long Mountain, whose majestic grandeur would in time elicit awe from my young nephew, Daniel, visiting for the first time from the hill-less Cayman Islands. His reaction was to sharply suck in a breath then loudly exclaim, "The mountain of the LORD my God!" (He had not long before seen *The Ten Commandments*).

Buoyed by the sparkling day and the miraculous success of the night before, we entered the University's administration building to request the chapel for our wedding. Everything else had gone so smoothly. Surely this would too.

We had expected to possibly hear that the date had already been taken. But a quick look showed that that was not the case. The first real hurdle was to prove that Selwyn was in truth a student at the university. Despite the fact that at the time he was registered with the UWI's Faculty of Science, somehow there was no record of him in the main administration's system nor in the very Science Faculty's records!

After an unsuccessful trip to the Faculty of Science, Selwyn was dejectedly on his way back to the Administration building, when he remembered the vision he had seen. He also recalled the account in the Scriptures of how the Israelites wandered for forty years in the desert because of unbelief and a whole generation missed the Promised Land. As he later recounted, he spun around and returned to the Faculty office, where one of his professors had just arrived. It was this professor who was able to sort through the computer problem and clarify that Selwyn was indeed a registered student of the university.

When he re-joined us with that news, yet another hurdle lay in front of us. The Chapel caretaker's leave began on that very day, December 28. That and the imminent

Christmas public holidays, were in fact the reasons the date had remained open. Undaunted, we asked the assistant what could be done to help us. She responded, almost as a joke, that our only hope was if we could get the caretaker to not go on leave that day. That was a tall order.

But we had seen GOD do some pretty incredible things so far, so we took the challenge, crossed UWI's famous Ring Road, and made a beeline for the chapel. The chapel's caretaker had already been alerted and, as he later explained, was preparing to deny our request. His plan had been to leave the city that morning to join a family event three hours away on the north coast on that very day.

When we entered the chapel, I noticed a surprised flash of recognition cross the caretaker's face. That was soon replaced by a welcoming smile. He recognized me! "Oh! It's you!" he said. When I responded with a stunned "yes." This was his reply, "I was preparing to say no, but if you will promise to be on time, since it's a morning wedding, I will stay and open up for you."

Of course, I would be on time, I assured him. We were overjoyed and effusive in our thanks. That's when he reminded me that he knew me well from all the times I had spent praying alone in the chapel or tinkering on the piano by the window.

I had taken refuge in the chapel many times during the wait when the doubts and anxiety were overwhelming. GOD was using my pain to bring me such pleasure. And isn't it also amazing that my wedding was set for the morning? Now look at GOD!

At 10:00 o'clock on the morning of Tuesday the 28th of December 1982, the University Chapel of the West Indies was filled from top to bottom with friends and family who, in the age before cell phones, email, or text messaging, miraculously had heard in time about this unusual wedding planned in nine days. (By the way, I later learned from a Jewish language student that Tuesday is a preferred day for weddings in their culture. I had always been a fan of Jewish culture, but did not know that. Look at GOD!)

We ended up with not one, but two wedding receptions all taken care of by our family and friends. The first, held immediately after the wedding ceremony, was a private family affair held at my Uncle's beautiful home near the chapel. The second, held two weeks later, was hosted by my friends in the University's Irvine Hall dining room. These beautiful moments did not cost us a red cent!

As a matter of fact, the wedding cake that we so generously distributed after our wedding was the extra cake from Janet's wedding, my friend who had gotten married on the 19th of December. Get this—my friend the groom, Christopher, is the son of a famous chef who at that time worked directly for Chris Blackwell. Christopher's mom had regularly served the likes of Bob Marley and other musical luminaries of the day. That December she was marrying off not one, but two of her sons, so she had "gone to town" baking them cakes. In Jamaica we say, "What drop offa head fall pon shoulder." I was the happy beneficiary of that windfall of wedding cake. I even had enough to follow the Jamaican tradition of freezing a small cake to eat on the first wedding anniversary!

And as for the gifts we thought that we would not have—in addition to a few gifts we received on the day of the wedding, two weeks after the wedding we had to hire a car to help us carry the load of gifts we received from one solitary couple. They had received many duplicate gifts at their own wedding some months earlier, so they invited us to their home and insisted we take them. And the gifts kept coming.

GOD proved that indeed HIS ways are higher than our ways and HIS thoughts higher than ours. HE was doing the "exceedingly abundantly, more than I could ask or imagine." HE had pulled off the wedding of my dreams without my having to lift a finger. Talk about no stress! Look at GOD!

We also did have a honeymoon. In fact, we "walk-footers" (meaning we didn't own a car and used public transportation) left for our North Coast, Ocho Rios honeymoon in a one-in-the-island, souped-up, custom-detailed, sky blue VW Bug with bold stripes reminiscent of the famous Herbie.

Selwyn's cousin, Denton, had graciously offered it to us. We were more than grateful, for Denton was very proud of his meticulously kept car. On top of that, he was trusting it to Selwyn who had never before driven outside of the city. What a blessing!

We had saved enough of our teachers' salary to be able to afford a few nights in a small hotel. Since we could only afford a few nights, we didn't balk when we had to cut our honeymoon short, in order for me to again minister with New Creation before year's end.

Do you remember my story about the New Year's Eve, Fishers of Men Banquet? The one where the LORD had told me to put the ring on my wedding finger, because by that time next New Year's Eve I would be married? Well guess what? That was the event at which our group was ministering.

That night also marked the first time Selwyn joined us on stage! And, this one took years before I made the connection, but I was also wearing the very ring that, at HIS word, I had moved over to my left hand that night. Only this time it had been sized to perfectly fit my finger! What a GOD!!

In case you are wondering, Selwyn did eventually get me a set of rings on one of our special anniversaries. It was a beautiful pair of rings that were made to nest in each other. When I got those, I retired the original ring.

Some years later, the "engagement ring" broke. I can't recall how, but we used the opportunity to make a custom band incorporating my mom's ring and Selwyn's new rings and diamonds. I wear these proudly to this day.

PART TWO

30

The School of Faith

S o, with a whirlwind of miracles to start your married life, how would you feel the coming years would be?

We felt that life was going to be great with absolutely no problems.

We would have children early,

travel the world singing for the LORD,

and preaching the gospel.

By the time we had settled into the rat-and-cockroach-infested garage flat that was all our paltry pay slips could provide, we were beginning to have a confrontation with reality. We had rented the flat from a kindly, elderly couple a few weeks after we were married. It would take a lot to make it feel like a home.

The problem was, we were two young high school teachers. Anybody who is a teacher knows that that is not the profession that brings home the big bucks. We had declined my parents' offer to have us live in our family home. We understood the love that prompted the suggestion, but we wanted to start life on our own.

Very soon it became clear we were not on our own. We had in fact enrolled in a course of miracles. We would have to undergo many tests in this school of faith. One comforting truth remained—the TEACHER was willing and able to guarantee our success.

31

The Promise

Within six months of being married two things happened:

We were told that it was going to be difficult for me to have children, because of what was eventually diagnosed as Polycystic Ovarian Syndrome.

The LORD confirmed to us that we would have children.

Suddenly, it was my turn to see visions. It was as clear as day. I saw a room chock full of stuff. Back then I did not focus on the stuff, for, seated on the floor with large, round eyes beaming up at me, and chortling gleefully was a precious baby boy. He had smooth bronzed skin and the most beautiful eyes. I was convinced I had seen my baby.

During my time of waiting for a baby, I was constantly having pregnancy symptoms. These were compounded by my wildly irregular menstrual periods. It was during one of those times that a name came to me.

I held it in my heart, anxiously watching and waiting to see if there was indeed a baby growing inside my womb. Not long after this, Selwyn came home from work one evening, and taking a look at my midsection, asked, "How's ....?", and he said the name. I jumped involuntarily. "How did you get that name?" I asked. He shrugged his shoulders and responded, "I don't know. It just came to me." At that, I opened up about the secret I had been carrying. We both agreed that now it would be our secret. We would tell no one else.

Now you need to understand that in our culture, as soon as one got married, the questions about how soon the baby could be expected would come pouring in. We got used to fielding them, and had soon felt led to answer truthfully that we were having difficulties. I distinctly recall the LORD's word to me. "Let them know you are having difficulties, so that when it happens, they will know that this is MY doing."

So it was not unusual to answer the question posed by my dear friend Judith who had come by for a visit. We were seated propped against pillows on our full-sized bed, which doubled as a sofa in the bedroom/living-room of our tiny garage flat. My answer to Judith's question was the usual. We were having difficulties conceiving, but we believed we would eventually have children. Before I moved on to other subjects, as was my usual modus operandi, I felt impressed to tell her the name of the child I had seen in the vision. That was odd, extremely odd.

I had always felt the LORD saying not to speak the name to anyone else. Why was I then having this strong urge and prompting to speak it? When I couldn't shake it, I told her about the vision and the name. Nothing could have prepared me for her response.

Judith began bouncing wildly on top of my bed, arms flailing, and shouting, "It's your baby! It's your baby!" Wide eyed, I waited for her to calm down. Then I asked what had evoked that unusual response. As she slowed her breathing, she explained that some months before, she had had a dream that was significant enough for her to share it with her roommates. She dreamed she was holding a baby, and someone had announced that his name was Jonathan.

Judith had herself been waiting on her own miracle. She was finally about to marry her childhood sweetheart and was waiting impatiently for the red tape of US immigration to allow her to join him there. Her friends teased her that maybe the baby was to be hers. She countered that this was a name for which she held no fondness. So, no. This was not her baby.

Now she was sure she knew whose it was. And we were then sure we had not made it all up. GOD had again spoken. And this was confirmation of HIS word. All this played out within the first year of our marriage.

Jehovah Jireh

Pretty soon we began to feel the constraints of our meager salaries. We had learnt earlier from some smart friends of ours, Al and Marjorie to be specific, how to use a budget. We also learned to place tithes and offerings in a place of priority. Good thing too, for we were about to prove the LORD's word about pouring out a blessing.

One particular month, I recall our tallying up all our expenses, comparing them to our income, and concluding that this would be a month when we would end up in the red. We proceeded gingerly through the weeks waiting for the proverbial shoe to drop. At the end of the month, the shoe was still in its place. It had still not descended. Quite to the contrary, we found ourselves with all our bills paid and our bank account showing a surplus of a whopping $50.00! (In our economy then, that felt like having US$500). The process of living on a tight budget tested and built our faith. We had many occasions of sitting on the edge of the financial precipice waiting to fall in, but never once going over.

It was during one of those times that GOD challenged me. I had commented on the lack of faith the disciples had shown, when, after the miraculous feeding of the three, and five thousand, they were filled with terror and panic on the storm-swept lake. "Imagine that!" I scoffed.

"A storm arose while they were in the boat with JESUS!"

"HE was in the boat with them."

"How could they be afraid?"

As I derided their lack of faith, the LORD spoke to me.

"Have I ever let you down?" Strange question in the midst of my holy rant.

But my quick response was "No."

HE then continued, "Why is it then, that every time you face a crisis, you act as if I have?"

It was another moment for me to blush in shame.

Here was I, so high-and-mightily judging those disciples, yet I too had been guilty of the same or worse lack of faith. I made a decision to trust GOD to be my provider. And that is when my eyes were opened to the miracles. I will share just one of the many miracles we experienced during that time.

33

Little Dutch Girl

I was sitting in a small group leaders' meeting when the young woman beside me asked if I would like some oranges. I thanked her kindly, and said yes, I would. She then shifted a bit uncomfortably and asked if I needed groceries. I, in turn, shifted very uncomfortably and said "yes." Just around that time, our supply of groceries was in fact dangerously low. She told me that she had some groceries in her car for me. How odd!

What was even more odd was that this young lady did not even own a car. Being a young Dutch missionary, she usually rode a bicycle everywhere she went. I could barely concentrate through the rest of the meeting. For, in addition to being just a bit embarrassed, I was also curious to solve this mystery.

After the meeting, she went to a car and opened the trunk to reveal a full box of groceries containing all the things that we were accustomed to buying, plus a few other "luxury" items. She confessed that the LORD had told her to go to the supermarket to buy these specific things, and that HE would show her later that evening who the recipient of the groceries should be. She had borrowed the car of a fellow missionary to carry the load!

As soon as she had settled herself in the seat beside me, the LORD had revealed to her that the groceries were for me. Her question about the oranges had been her way of testing the waters. What a good thing I had not allowed my pride to make me decline her offer!

As she uncovered the box and displayed its contents, I noticed two items of groceries that still stand out to me. They were the *bun and cheese.* As our friendship deepened, Carin later told me that some of the items on the list had puzzled her, because in her culture it was not usual to eat savory and sweet together.

We are amused that after sharing bun and cheese with me on many occasions, it has become one of her favorite food choices. She's even been known to have it for breakfast! (Something no self-respecting Jamaican does.) GOD was showing us big time that HE was our true source—not our job. HE was our FATHER in the truest sense of the word. Go GOD!

34

Career Twists

Recently, I reread, a bit of Joseph's story in the Bible, and it dawned on me that he was actually led kicking and screaming to the fulfillment of his dreams. That certainly made me stop to think about my own life. Of course, I haven't reached the heights of Joseph by any stretch of the imagination, but hopefully you get my point. We don't always recognize when GOD is leading us towards our desired place. This was the case with me in the world of work.

I may not have mentioned that my long-held dream was to marry, have a family (two boys and two girls) and stay home to raise them. I know that doesn't fit into the narrative of the women's liberation movement and other modern ideologies. And for those who know how fiercely I fight against women's place being dictated by men; it may come as a shock that I was embracing such a traditional role. But there it was. I had a choice, and I would make it. This was the choice for me. I like the simplicity, and power even, of closely interacting with and influencing my family from within the home.

I had shared this desire with Selwyn, and he had grown to accept the idea. With that in mind, as soon as we had stepped over the three-month threshold as a newly wedded couple, (naïvely, I now believe) I was ready to start our family.

Why three months you ask? Because I was conscious that for some people, our speedy wedding could have been interpreted as a sign that I was covering up a pre-wedding pregnancy. The problem, however, was that the children would not come. That is its own story. In the meantime, I busied myself in the world of work. I continued to teach Spanish at Immaculate Conception High School (ICHS).

It was on the way to work one morning, while we waited together to catch our separate buses, that Selwyn suddenly turned to look at me and declared that he had just had a vision of me all dressed up and working in a technical field. This was at best, laughable, because I was the student who was allowed to drop Mathematics at O'Levels (11th grade) in a school where Math was compulsory.

The principal himself had suggested it, so that I wouldn't waste my poor teacher-mother's money. At that point, both my younger brother and I were set to sit the expensive overseas exams at the same time. His intervention was an act of mercy, since there was no way that, with a six or nine percent (I can't remember which) average and a report card that said "Diane tries!" I would have passed the exams. Technical subjects required Math. Nope. Selwyn was mistaken this time.

On top of that, according to him, the image of me he saw was fancily dressed, hair straightened, and wearing makeup! Once again, let's apply some context. I was the girl who despised makeup. I believed my face as GOD made it never needed embellishment, so much so that at my wedding, my girlfriends had to insist on being allowed to put on a barely-there eyeliner and the equally invisible Transparent Burgundy lipstick. My poor mother also lost the battle to have my hair straightened for the occasion. I was adamant that Selwyn would marry me just as I was. So again, this image of future me was truly ludicrous.

141

I spent a lovely three years at ICHS, where I thoroughly enjoyed sharing life with the young ladies who were in my charge. Sadly, I am a person who gets bored easily if things follow a predictable cycle. I know most people enjoy opening up an exam to find the same question they had previously aced looking back at them. Unfortunately, I am not one of those people. For me that is a sure-fire way to earn a less than stellar grade. And that became my problem as a high school teacher of Spanish.

If you ever had the privilege of a modern language education at the University of the West Indies, you know that they do an excellent job of preparing you for using the language in the real world. In truth, had I moved directly into a job translating or interpreting the language, I would have at that time found myself very equal to the challenge. I was also freshly studied up on the great masters of Spanish literature. This meant that, as was the case, when in high school I was taught by recent university graduates, I would be more closely connected to the material, and better able to teach it to my students.

In the world of traditional education though, without a degree in education, I was considered a novice. For that reason, I was only allowed to teach mostly rudimentary Spanish language and grammar. Before long, my Spanish vocabulary dwindled to the very basics, and I knew all the exercises and on what page the various lessons could be found in the textbooks. Simply put, I became bored.

At least I thought that was the reason for my growing unease and restlessness. Looking back at how much I enjoyed all the relationships I formed at ICHS (many still intact today) and the satisfaction I derived from sharing life with my students, I seriously wonder if boredom was my real reason for resigning. I now see the hand of GOD like the eagle stirring up the nest and making it uncomfortable for me to stay. GOD was the eagle prodding me to go.

After praying about it and getting Selwyn's buy in, I tendered my resignation. Strangely, or some may say foolishly, I had not even attended another job interview. I simply left, because I felt it was time. I asked the LORD for a one-month holiday, after which I was prepared to begin working somewhere else. In truth, I didn't have a place in mind. I recall I toyed with the idea of working in a department store. I thought it would have been refreshing to liaise with the stream of diverse people I imagined would pass through the store's doors.

Well, the LORD had other ideas. From the few feelers I eventually put out among my parents' circle of friends and acquaintances, the common response was that I, with a university degree, was overqualified for that sort of job. So, it was once again a GOD thing, when, at exactly a month after tendering my resignation, my mom visited our apartment to ask if I thought I could fill in for a friend of hers at the Language Training Centre. I would work as a teacher of English as a Second Language (TESOL), and I would be teaching adults from varying language backgrounds. Now that sounded interesting!

When I went for the interview, I discovered that apart from my mom's friend's classes, there were other classes needing a teacher. I was offered the position on the spot. Having taken the job, I soon realized that I needed different skills teaching adults. One of them was to look like an adult. After all, some of my students were old enough to be my parent.

I don't think I mentioned before, that by the time I was married, I had managed to pack on enough pounds to say goodbye to my usual 83lb self. In keeping with being numerically challenged, I don't remember if it was 90 or 95 pounds of me that fit into my used wedding dress. All that to say that I vividly recall my fat crisis when, not long after marriage, I bulked up to a whopping 107lbs. In the real world, however, that, combined with my fresh face and natural hairdos, did very little to give me the stature and air of confident experience that said, "I am adult. Hear me teach."

As I experimented with ways of appearing older, I reluctantly straightened my hair, paid more attention to my outfits, and cautiously ventured into the world of makeup. It was at the Language Training Centre that I first met and fell in love with Panamanians. At that time many of them came to Jamaica to learn English. Quite a few were in my classes.

After a while, I began to have a steady stream of private clients that included diplomats and their families. That's when Selwyn's vision came back to me—the one he had received some years before in our very early marriage. I pointed out to him that I was now dressing up, using makeup, and dealing with "important" clients, so maybe this was the vision fulfilled. He curtly declared that this was not that.

"You were in charge in a technical field, and the men you were dealing with were Scandinavian!"
If I didn't roll my eyes to his face, I certainly did it inwardly.

After a few years teaching at the Language Training Centre, a colleague approached me. Once again, I was being asked to fill in for someone going on leave. The institution she mentioned was one I had, up till then, never heard of. It was the Jamaica Maritime Training Institute (JMTI)—a government project aimed at developing Jamaicans for positions on commercial shipping vessels. How interesting!

My colleague, Elinor Felix, had been responsible for teaching all the English language classes there. As she drove me to the Palisadoes strip where the Institute was located, she tried her best to explain to me how this very-well-hidden institute operated. They were providing International-Maritime-Organization certified training to their students. English and Spanish were additional offerings, but not necessary for the certificates. I learned that the Language Training Centre had been contracted to provide teachers for those courses. And I learned that if I liked it, and they liked me, the job would be permanently mine, since she was in fact not going on leave, but moving to another job elsewhere. To cut a long story very short, I soon became the official language teacher at the JMTI.

35

Deep Waters

It didn't take me long to realize that I was in deep waters literally and figuratively. Not being the owner of a car, I soon learned two very useful things:

There was a ferry leaving from the wharf downtown that took people to and from the Institute on weekdays.

The ferry was probably the only thing in Jamaica that ran exactly on time.

(I may have had them reverse to allow me on board at the last minute once or twice. And I may have missed it a few times. Who's counting? Not me.)

Once again, I had students who were my seniors. By then that did not faze me. The maritime world was decidedly male dominated. That in itself did not faze me either. I met some of the loveliest gentlemen there, but at times it felt like this little spit of land in a corner of the Palisadoes strip was where chauvinism had come to reign. Growing up in a family with a dad and three brothers, and having attended co-ed schools all my life, I soon learned to swim with the big boys.

As the years passed, what did finally wear me down, however, was the fact that there was little regard for the subjects I taught, since no one really needed them in order to be internationally certified. I eventually lost interest in preparing lessons for a mostly uninterested group of students. One year, before the summer break, I notified them that I would not be returning.

At the same time that I was again becoming unemployed, New Creation released their first recorded album. True to my desire to sing for the LORD "full time", I grasped at the free time as an opportunity to promote and manage the group. I was busily engaged in setting myself up to work in the makeshift home office some friends had loaned the group, when I received the call.

There was to be a new director at the Institute. He was requesting that I come to meet with him. More out of curiosity than anything else, I made the trip to see him. Without preamble, he indicated that he had noticed me on a previous visit to the Institute and wished me to rejoin the staff. I explained my frustration with the way things had been, and he assured me that he would seek ways to engage me in meaningful activities.

With that, I grudgingly acquiesced and returned to my teaching position. Because I had disclosed to him my involvement in promoting our group, and because my position was still part time, I was able to use some of my free time to continue to do work on behalf of the group. This eventually came to an end in the most startling way.

One year, I noticed a visitor to the Institute who was engaged in meetings with the administrative team. I could only guess at the technicalities of their discussions. Much to the chagrin of my students, even after many years there, I had barely begun to learn to refer to the vessels they commanded as ships instead of boats.

So, it was quite unexpected when I was approached by this Frenchman to meet with him to discuss a proposal. Again, it was my aroused curiosity that made me head to the conference room to sit opposite him. After introducing himself as a representative of a UN training program aimed at the land-based shipping industry, he proceeded to ask me to be responsible for establishing it in Jamaica and the English-speaking Caribbean.

I interrupted to remind him that I had absolutely no background in shipping, that I was merely the English and Spanish teacher. Undaunted, he proceeded to explain all that setting up the program entailed and seemed to be sure I was the person who could do it. Finally, I asked, "Did the director ask you to speak with me?" When he said yes, I decided to hear him out then take it up with the director, which is what I did.

Rudolf Rist, with a twinkle in his eye, revealed that he had in fact asked Raymond Byl to speak with me. He explained that he was aware of my frustration with my teaching duties and believed I was more than able to handle this project.

In fact, at his prodding, some years before I had stepped out of my normal work routine by coordinating the World Maritime University's Conference for Central American and Caribbean Graduates. Another time I was able to help organize the International Labor Organization's Conference on Caribbean Maritime Labor Standards. I had thoroughly enjoyed every minute of those opportunities. But, I argued, that was about organizing and coordinating. This was going to need knowledge of the industry. Mr. Rist was unflinching. He felt I was equal to the task.

Bolstered by the confidence both men displayed in my abilities, and relieved to embrace a real challenge, I accepted. Paired with this came a deep dread that I was walking outside of the will of GOD, as surely, there would be no more time left to give attention to the music group's affairs. I had also naïvely held the opinion that the only worthwhile work was work of a spiritual nature. GOD, I erroneously thought, could not be interested in the banal world of international commerce.

This new position would entail some travel, and the first of these trips was to the Norwegian Shipping Academy where I would be exploring the feasibility of a joint project involving the teaching of Maritime English. This was my first business trip, and I was excited to venture into another country. It was also my first time seeing snow on the ground.

Once again, I couldn't shake the feeling of dread that I was totally outside the will of GOD. For what eternal significance could this type of business hold? It was this despair that enveloped me, as I sat on the edge of the bed in my hotel room in Norway. I had moved past the excitement of travel and my first glimpse of snow. All that then filled my heart was a sadness over being caught up in the mundane affairs of the world and being estranged from the things that mattered to GOD.

As I allowed the feeling to wash over me, I heard the now familiar voice of GOD.

"Where are you?"

"Norway," came my confused response.

"But, where are you?" HE insisted.

"Scandinavia," I responded

"And why are you here?" HE continued.

"Business," I said, suddenly sensing a trend.

"But what kind of business?"

With my response "Technical business," the penny dropped.

Instantly I was awash with the awesome presence of GOD. Here I was allowing my religious preconceptions to convince me I had walked away from the will of GOD for my life, when I was sitting smack dab in the middle of the fulfillment of a vision, HE had given to my husband 10 years before!

I was indeed all dressed up and doing business in a technical field with Scandinavian men! GOD was blowing my mind on so many levels. HIS word was rock solid. And though it tarries, we should never doubt its fulfillment. We should wait for it.

Habakkuk 2:3 could not have said it more clearly. "This vision is for a future time. It describes the end, and it will be fulfilled. If it seems slow in coming, wait patiently, for it will surely take place. It will not be delayed."

This was a lesson that would have far-reaching consequences, as I waited for the fulfillment of another word—the promised children. I was now certain that GOD would do what HE said. And HE would do it in HIS time.

With GOD's stamp of approval, I delved deeper into the maritime waters, helping to establish the Institute as the Regional United Nations Conference on Trade and Development (UNCTAD) Trainmar Centre, the official training arm of the Caribbean Shipping Association, and eventually the provider of the region's only Diploma in Shipping Logistics. The Institute's change of name from "Jamaican" to "Caribbean," as well as its dropping "Training" from its name was born from this effort. So deep was my dive that, for the first time since leaving the University of the West Indies, I was motivated to pursue further studies.

For those who may balk at my lack of scholarly ambition, I hasten to clarify that I did pursue the odd training course for professional development over the years. But I'm not ashamed to say I was never a fan of studying. I would only do it if I truly needed to.

Before setting the diploma in place, I had gathered a solid team of young shipping professionals who had all pursued shipping education and training outside of the region. They were the mainstay that provided the instruction for the Trainmar courses I organized. We were a dynamic team.

When I considered the diploma program, however, I realized that I could not reasonably be responsible for managing course developers and subject matter experts without having an in-depth knowledge of the material myself. With that, I did something I had vowed never to do. I enrolled in a program of study that would have me separate from my husband for many months.

36

The GOD Who Sees

The year was 1993. I became an international scholarship student in a small, remote town in northern Holland. I was the first from Jamaica to attend the International Maritime Training Academy. I had made the journey alone to this cold country leaving my husband in our sunny apartment in our Jamaican island home. I was to be away for eight months. I had been away from Selwyn often on my numerous business trips, but the longest we had ever been apart was three weeks. I had made this journey to chilly Holland on the promise that, should the separation ever become too much for me,

Selwyn would come to join me till my studies were complete.

Those were the days of letters, stamps, and post offices. The fax machine was cutting edge technology and astounded me, as I tried to wrap my mind around my handwriting flying across the miles and appearing on a paper somewhere else exactly as I had sent it.

My small college had no fax machines available for students. It had no telephones in the homes that served as dormitories to us, the foreign students from across the globe. Our only opportunity to connect with our families was a phone at the end of a narrow corridor outside the small administrative cubicles that served as the faculty hub of our tiny college.

Also, the fact that we were many miles away from home meant that we were also time zones apart from our loved ones at home. Phone connectivity meant planning. We had to prearrange times to be standing near the phone on the wall, so we could receive the call from home. As you may imagine, those calls were not very frequent. Many letters crossed the miles between us.

Well, it was during this time of prolonged separation that GOD taught me the lesson of HIS omnipresence— nearer than breathing, closer than my next breath. Little by little, I began to appreciate the fact that GOD's Presence created a bond between Selwyn and me. It started with simple things like Selwyn and I "coincidentally" reviewing the same passage of Scripture, or having the same song on repeat in our heads, or having the same thoughts, as we watched the moon in the night sky knowing that for me it was almost morning, and for him it was midnight.

We would remark on this new phenomenon in the letters that crossed the miles to each other. But the clincher, the one that settled it for us that our GOD was very present in both our worlds and keeping us connected to each other, happened over one unusually sunny weekend.

In September of 1993 a group of about 20 international students converged on the small, remote navy town of Den Helder. We had each left loved ones behind but were a bit reticent to make new friend-connections. From my journey from near introversion to friendliness, I had learned that many who seemed aloof were in reality only shy and uncertain of how to break the ice. Having had many years of practice since my 19-year old self had received the "get-your-act-together" talk from my two-and-a-half-year-younger little sister, and having successfully put my smiling and conversational skills to good use over many years, I set out to help the other strangers feel more settled in our new temporary home. Little did I know, this was about to backfire.

His name was Christian. He had arrived late into our orientation period and had seemed a bit lost. Sticking my arm out and flashing my smile, I introduced myself and welcomed him to our group. Yes, he was a man, but I was used to a father, three brothers, and a host of male friends. The opposite sex did not scare me. On top of all that, we were married folk with our heartthrobs waiting for us at home.

Well, that was a handshake I lived to regret. In short order I started to notice that Christian's friendliness exceeded the normal limits. With that, I began to find ways to avoid him and was glad his dorm was across the bridge on the other side of our little town.

It came to a head, however, the day I stayed home from classes because of an illness. I was startled to find that a whole bunch of flowers had made their way to our dormitory addressed to me from Christian. Having become aware of what was clearly an inappropriate interest in me on his part, I left the flowers in our shared living room, where all my flat mates could enjoy them.

Since I was one of only two women who shared our flat, it had been established that she would be the only visitor allowed in my third-floor bedroom. We all socialized in the public space on the second floor. So, that sunny Saturday evening when I heard the knock on my bedroom door, I didn't hesitate to say "come in". After all, it had to be my other female flat mate.

Well, you guessed it. It wasn't. Looming large in the doorframe of my minuscule dorm room, looking down on the bed on which I was sitting was none other than Christian! Why was he here in our house? And why was he in my room? Who had sent him up our steep attic stairs? While I was plotting to give whoever did this a good piece of my mind, I suddenly became aware of an alarming emotion.

I was beginning to physically respond to this man's presence in my room. As a matter of fact, I became acutely aware that Christian had not entered my room alone. There were definitely seducing spirits that had accompanied him.

Flustered, but on my guard, I began to pray desperately under my breath, pretending to be at ease but panicking inside. I quickly drew his attention to my wall of fame where I had stuck photos of all my family including very prominent ones of Selwyn. I feigned nonchalance, as I recounted little anecdotes about each photo. Inwardly I screamed, "HOLY SPIRIT, help me!" Not long after that, he turned to leave, and I crumpled to the bed, a heap of confusion, but so thankful and relieved that it was finally over.

As I replayed the scene many times in my mind over the rest of the weekend, I came to the grim realization that this was a spiritual battle the likes of which I had never faced before. Never before had I felt so powerless in the face of an unwanted advance. Had the HOLY SPIRIT not intervened, I would not have been able to resist this man!

I couldn't wait for my scheduled Monday afternoon call from Selwyn. I would have to find a way to not alarm him, as I let him know I nearly lost control with another man. As soon as we said "hello" and "how are you?", it was Selwyn who cut to the chase. "Diane," he said, "what happened on Saturday at about 3 p.m. your time?"

Shocked, I quickly blurted out the whole sorry tale. But uppermost in my mind was why he had even asked the question in the first place. His response floored me. "At about 3 p.m. your time on Saturday, I had an urgent impulse to pray for you, so I did until the feeling left not long afterwards, and I was at peace. Now I know why."

I was flooded with relief. Even though many miles separated us, the HOLY SPIRIT was binding us together and made Selwyn respond to my cry for help. I could rest in the knowledge that, though we were apart, GOD, the omniscient, was looking out for me in the meantime.

No Man's Debtor

Some years before I made my move to the maritime world, Selwyn had decided to branch out and lend his abilities to another field. This was the competitive world of life insurance. It was there that GOD again tested our trust in him to provide.

In addition to being a pastor, my dad had also sold life insurance. His Million-Dollar-Round-Table [MDRT] emblazoned "knights-of-the-round-table" beer mugs were proud testimony to his status in the industry. That status, though, had come at a price. The industry demanded premium time. Many evenings we ate at the large mahogany table without our father at its head. It was customary for his meal (the best portions) to be shared out and kept for his habitual late arrival home.

At that time, we children would gather at the table again to watch him eat while regaling us with stories or teasing us mercilessly. If we were lucky, he would leave us a portion of his meal, which was usually a well-mixed me-lee of pieces of meat, gravy and whatever the carbs were. He tried to make up for his absence with frequent family road trips and the like, but as I grew older, I could see the strain on our mother. It was clear she wanted more of him in the daily grind. This was why I had sworn to never marry an insurance salesman.

Selwyn, after moving from teaching to the slightly more lucrative data processing world, found himself still unset-tled in a career. Although he had been an excellent teacher, he could not support a family on its wages. He en-joyed the structures and organizational skills to which data processing introduced him. But, he soon found that he had arrived at the pinnacle with no more room for growth. That was when he decided, on the advice of his boss, to con-sider a career in life insurance.

To say I was disappointed is putting it mildly. However, as we prayed about it, and Selwyn reminded me of how he had taken a chance on my career change when I had left

ICHS; I could do nothing more than to give in and trust GOD.

Selwyn was a natural. My dad was forced to openly declare his admiration and confess his earlier misgivings, when Selwyn himself was now qualifying for the MDRT year after year. I, myself, had to admit that he had made an excellent decision. Through his eyes, I developed a new respect for the industry.

After only a few years of selling life insurance, he shocked us all by becoming a Unit Manager. That was quite an achievement. It was shortly after this, that I went to study in Holland. When I had received the scholarship, I accepted based on Selwyn's promise that, should I ever need him, he would be there.

I always describe that particular time in Holland as comparable to being accustomed to moving around in a dark room, then having someone come and turn on a light, stay just enough for you to become accustomed to it, then leave and take the light with them. That is how I felt when Selwyn returned to Jamaica, after having spent the Christmas holidays with me in Holland.

When he left, the lights in my world went out, and no matter how many candles I tried to light by telling myself, to get it together and act like a grown up, I was falling apart. I had to make the call. As he later told me, the call came shortly after he had received a promotion to the position of Assistant Branch Manager. He had a crucial decision to make.

Having discussed it with family and colleagues, he was told that to leave at that time would be to commit career suicide. But over the almost 11 years of our marriage, the LORD had taught him to put the needs of family first and trust HIM to provide. He took the decision to join me in the final two months of my studies.

GOD's timing was impeccable, because it seemed like almost every subject in that course contained some element of math. Had Selwyn not arrived on April 1, 1994, in time to tutor me through the rigors of the math-infused material, I doubt I would have successfully completed the course.

While in Holland with me, Selwyn was able to receive one faxed report from his agents in Jamaica. It showed that, even in his absence, the unit was doing well. When he returned to work in June, he was informed that during his absence, his unit of salespeople had performed so well, that they had outperformed all other units and even some branch offices throughout the island. On the strength of that successful performance, he was promoted to the position of Branch Manager.

GOD is no man's debtor. Selwyn's decision to put family first did not result in the expected demotion. On the contrary, it was rewarded with a promotion!

I joined the prophet Jeremiah in declaring, "Ah, LORD GOD! Behold, YOU have made the heavens and the earth by YOUR great power and outstretched arm. There is nothing too hard for YOU" (Jeremiah 32:17).

PART THREE

38

Children...

As the years passed, we kept a steady lookout for the promised child. We did all the medical things that people who were having difficulty having children did:

All the medical visits,

All the tests,

All the fertility drugs that I took till my hair began to thin, and I literally was seeing stars.

We even took advantage of Selwyn's time in Holland to, together, consult Dutch medical fertility specialists in the hope of finally being able to conceive the promised child.

Whenever Mothers' Day came, it got more and more difficult for me, as the years passed with no children in sight. It was compounded by all the greetings and assurances that even though I had no children of my own, I was "a mother in Zion." How I hated that term!

But, the LORD kept sending people to us to let us know that we would have children. In the very early years of our marriage, HE even had me purchase a complete set of baby bottles as a sign of my trust in HIM. I had trusted HIM when I bought it. But, as the years rolled on, and others around me were having their own children, I had to often fight the urge to pull the set from my drawer, wrap it up, and present it as a gift to the next "blessed and highly favored" mother-to-be. (If you sense sarcasm, it's because that's how I felt.)

My dear friend Marjorie saw my deep sadness. She knew I had dreams of one day having a son called Jonathan and a daughter called Joanna. When she delivered a daughter, her third child, she decided to name her Joanna and make us her godparents. With that name taken, we knew we would have to find another name for the daughter we hoped GOD would send us.

It was a hard road. I recall my deep disappointment, as every significant year rolled by. A baby didn't come in year three, not year five, not even year seven—the number of completion. After year ten, the year I had seen the fulfillment of the vision given to Selwyn in our first year of marriage, I finally broke before GOD. That's when I began to grasp the idea that my concept of time was vastly different from GOD's.

Acceptance

It was an evening after work. I was alone in my car wrestling with my disappointment. That's when the question came. "Will you accept whatever I have for you?" I groaned with a sadness too deep for words. I longed for children. But I had also seen the hand of GOD so vividly displayed in my life. I knew I would have to allow HIM to do whatever HE wished. My head said yes, but my heart was breaking into tiny shards, each one piercing irreparable holes into the fabric of my dreams. This was where I decided. I decided to tell my heart to trust again.

I recalled the song I had composed standing in the shower in our first year of marriage. I had just been diagnosed with dysfunctional uterine bleeding. The clumps of evidence ran down my legs and mingled with the water from the shower. As I stood drenched in misery, the Enemy began to taunt me. "You are bleeding out your child. Curse GOD"

Out of nowhere strength rose up within me, and I began to put a melody to words from the book of Job adding some of my own. "For though YOU slay me, yet will I trust YOU, for even in death I'll glorify YOU. And my life is giving glory to YOUR name." As I repeated the phrase through my tears, the Enemy took his leave.

So, that evening many years later, through blinding tears, I finally settled it again. I was again deciding to say yes to whatever HE had for my life. I realized that, deep down; I had not trusted HIM enough to accept whatever HE had in store for me, even if it meant no children.

That would have to change. As the tears overflowed, and my choking sobs exploded, I began to sing my acceptance:

"I'll say yes, LORD."

By the time I had sung it a few times, the tears had melted away the painful lump in my throat. It washed away

any remaining stumbling block to trusting GOD in this matter. I was rewarded with a peace that made me know that,
with or without children, it would be well. I would praise
HIM in the meantime.

40

A Prophet and an Angel?

Adding to my misery that day, was another promise I had received from the LORD. In the eighth year of our marriage, our singing group, New Creation, was a guest at a Charismatic Teaching Conference. After we sang in one of the sessions, the guest speaker, Dr Myles Munroe, went to the pulpit. Before starting his message, he looked into the audience and asked me to come to the platform, so I did. He asked that my husband come also, so Selwyn joined me. Then he said to me, "You are having an ovary problem, but you will have children, children that sing."

You may just be able to grasp a bit of the uproar that ensued during and after this prophecy. The crowd surged around us at the end of the meeting, many touching my tummy. The next day we had to answer the wildly inappropriate question that kept being repeated, "So, did you guys put the baby in last night?" My goodness!

Now it seemed the whole world was badgering us about the children that were very slow in coming. I now have confirmation that the date of that word from Dr Myles Munroe was August 5, 1990. I am sure, because it was Devie's 13th birthday. Being one of my "favorite daughters," she had never forgotten, and recently she reminded me. She was one of those who had waited along with me.

This publicity had, unknown to me, brought a whole host of other people alongside us, supporting us in prayer during our mean time. We all waited and waited, and at least once per year the LORD would remind us of HIS promise. Someone would have a dream, a vision, or a word of encouragement. It was the dream that would not let us go. And, if I'm honest, I had many days where again I thought that maybe we had all been misled.

Then, after approximately 13 years of marriage and many years of medical treatment, one evening we stopped at a local supermarket where we frequently shopped.

Standing at the entrance was an old woman, whom we had never seen before. She appeared to be a beggar, so I decided to offer her some money before she asked. She took it and thanked me.

I entered the supermarket, did my shopping, and began to head to my car. As I was leaving, the old woman again approached me. I have to confess to being annoyed, because I thought that she was going to ask for more money.

Instead, to my surprise, she asked if I had children. Inwardly I rolled my eyes and thought, "Not again!" Somehow people always asked. Outwardly I faked a smile and responded that I did not. To my amazement, she proceeded to say to me that she would pray to the LORD that by next year this time, I would have a baby boy. I was speechless!

After I stumbled back to my car, Selwyn and I marveled at the strange occurrence. We asked each other if we had ever seen that woman before on our previous visits to this neighborhood store. We agreed that we had not. In all our subsequent trips to that supermarket, we never ever saw her again. We concluded that the woman must have been an angel, and that once again we had received a promise from the LORD.

41

Promise Keeper

One year after meeting that old lady, seven years after the conference, and fourteen-and-a-half years after being married the LORD blessed us with a baby boy. We named him Jonathan. And his most striking feature has been his big, beautiful, shining eyes.

When we brought him before the congregation to be blessed, nothing prepared us for the outpouring of love and praise to our LORD in thanks for his birth. It turns out that many who had been witness to the prophecy of his coming had been badgering GOD over the years to see it come to pass. We had not been fighting our prayer battles alone.

For many, our story was a sign that GOD would fulfill the promises HE had made to them too. We had seen that before, when I had been led to tell some people about our wedding date. Our story had become a part of their promise. We were evidence of GOD's amazing faithfulness to perform HIS word. Oh, the beauty of the Body of CHRIST! Look at GOD!

Remember the girl named Thursday? Not long ago while going through some old keepsakes, I found another Aba treasure. It was her notes from my baby shower, before Jonathan was born. She had been again mothering me.

She had gathered my friends and family and prepared a list. This time she was making sure I had the answers to the "what if's" of successfully managing a newborn. She was among the many who rejoiced with me at the fulfillment of GOD's word.

Hebrews 10:23 of the New King James Version (NKJV) says, "Let us hold fast the confession of our hope without wavering, for He who promised is faithful."

Although I thoroughly enjoyed my work in the Caribbean shipping industry, I was happy to finally leave the world of work to live the long-awaited dream of being a mother at home. I happily traded the title of Director,

Training and Marketing for the title Home Manager. (That's right, "Housewife" does not sit well with me. I'm wife to a husband, not a house. OK, rant over.)

The year after Jonathan was born, we again encountered Myles Munroe at another of the annual charismatic teaching conferences. As we proudly introduced him to Jonathan and captured the moment in a photo, he teased, "Remember the word was children, not child!" We had not forgotten, but we were stunned that he had remembered!

Jason came 20 months after Jonathan, and our daughter a little over two years after Jason. Since we were already "parents" to our Joanna, we searched and found a similar name for our new daughter.

We named her Jovanna, our "GOD is gracious" to us. And gracious she was. She is the only baby I'm aware of that one could safely awaken from a nap and be rewarded with a warm smile instead of howls of disapproval. I was happy to show her off to the many visitors that welcomed a princess to our family.

Not one of the births was planned (at least not by us.) Over several years, we had pursued various medical treatments. We had even done a laparoscopic wedge resection, while we were in Holland. We finally saw results following an open ovarian wedge resection in Jamaica. After that, it seemed we couldn't stop the children from coming. There's a spiritual lesson right there.

All the members of the body are important. Without my ovaries functioning correctly, none of my other reproductive and child-nurturing organs had any chance of fulfilling their purpose. As soon as that one malfunction was corrected, the others were all released to their destiny. How wise it is that GOD calls the Church one Body!

Out of concern for my health, despite my initial protestations, all my children were delivered by C-section, and my tubes were tied after the third one. Although I was a happy mother, I harbored some sadness at not having had the experience of a natural birth, nor the possibility of having a second daughter. Even there, the hand of the LORD was leading. That though, is its own story.

Again, we saw GOD's faithfulness. As the children grew, we were happy to note that GOD had not only given us children, as HE had promised, but he had also given us "children that sing!" I had seen first-hand what 1 Thessalonians 5:24 reminds us, "He who calls you is faithful, who also will do it."

PART FOUR

42

The Best-Planned Accident

So there we finally were—the parents of three toddlers: a five-year old, a three-year old and a one-year old. By then Selwyn was employed in the corporate world. I, having given up on my dream of homeschooling my children, was busy at home with my baby girl all day and my young boys in the afternoon when they returned from their separate kindergartens.

Jonathan was attending a small school a few streets away from where we lived. It was my consolation prize. It was the one closest to a homeschool—small, and aiming for academic excellence. Jonathan was happily settled after his initial extended orientation period:

The one where I would sit outside his classroom where he could see me. The one where I endured the pity and disapproval of staff and parents alike, while I waited for him to release me to leave for home, after he finally adjusted his mind to the fact that he would spend the morning learning with these strange people instead of teaching me at home. (And yes. You heard right. This son of mine thought he was the teacher.)

Jason used to be in another classroom, one without an eyeshot of the tree under which I would wait. I would hear him wailing, demanding to be released from his strange prison. Despite all the assurances from the staff that he would be fine and eventually adjust, he didn't.

I would return at 11a.m. to collect a weepy child who had not settled all morning. Jonathan eventually settled but not Jason. So, I did what I had to.

I moved Jason to Rainbow Land. It was not tiny like a homeschool. But Jason loved it. And the teachers and parents encouraged me to sit and wait for him to feel at home. And when he did, all too quickly, they invited me to sit in his circles and watch him bloom.

I had my baby girl with me. We would sometimes sit together in Jason's learning circles or play in the schoolyard beneath the approving gaze of the teachers, before we finally made it home to do whatever a mom of a baby girl with two not-much-older brothers does before it's pickup time. I believe it may have involved playing with an orange-colored, plastic, bear-shaped baby bottle. Remember the baby bottle set that had been with me all those years as my tangible assurance that GOD would fulfill HIS word? I eventually used the glass ones for supplemental feedings of my three babies. The plastic one became their toy.

So yes, Jonathan was in one school. Jason was in another, and Jovanna, my soon-to-be two-year old, was at home with me. Selwyn was totally immersed in his project at the Jamaica Money Market Brokers Limited (JMMB).

Immersed I say, but in truth, he would barely come up for air. This company thrived on excellence, creativity, and hard work. There were meetings and deadlines. He was spearheading a project to introduce a new concept—insurance for their growing client base.

In keeping with our long-held tradition of helping each other in our various work projects, it was all hands on deck, as soon as we put the children to bed. We pulled many an all-nighter to churn out PowerPoint presentations that aimed to sell the concept first to the internal market, before it could be launched to the customer base. It was tough going, but we were not afraid of tough. We were people who got the job done.

So, there we were, having pulled back-to-back all-nighters, trying to decide how we would organize our family to attend a wedding and a funeral many miles apart on the same day. We decided to divide and conquer. Selwyn would take the children in Lucy (our ultra-comfortable, miracle, family van) to the happy event. He would be helped by our friend who sometimes babysat our children and who also happened to be a guest at the same wedding and needed a ride. Perfect!

I would attend the sad event. I would hitch a ride with friends to commiserate with my dear friend, Marie, at her dad's funeral. We would all meet at home in the evening to fill each other in on what we had missed from our separate days out.

At the end of the day, on the ride back into the city, from the backseat of Tal and Denise's SUV, I simultaneously engaged in conversation with my drivers and with Selwyn. The magic of cell-phones would make it possible for me to receive updates on where Selwyn was on his route and his estimated time of arrival at home.

As it turned out, we pulled into our driveway only seconds behind each other. He had beaten us to it and was parking the van in the raised carport. I remained in the SUV parked below in our driveway finishing up the conversation that had been sparked, when our dear friends of many years finally discovered that the mutual friend at whose parties we often met was, in fact, my younger brother, Bruce.

As we were laughing at how they had thought to pro-tect me from the sometimes-inappropriate outbursts that were not uncommon at those gatherings, I called to Selwyn to come join us to laugh at this new revelation. When he came alongside the car, with Jason, my social one, in tow, I took the opportunity to go greet the rest of my family who had spent an entire day away from me.

When we had bought our van, we had been advised that, after a long journey, we should let it throttle for a while before shutting it off. This was in order to preserve the turbo diesel engine. For that reason, the engine had not been turned off, when Selwyn came out to greet us.

As the sitter was taking stuff from the car, I noticed the van begin to move. I was beside it, but not yet near enough to get into it. Jonathan and Jovanna were still inside the vehicle. I watched, as my sitter friend made a quick exit. Then my eyes switched to slow motion mode.

I see Jonathan sitting in the back row. I see the car slowly roll back. I see Jason standing with his dad beside our friends' car door. I see their laughter congeal on their faces, as their eyes widen. I see Jason's head in line with what was sure to become the impact zone. I see Selwyn turn around to face the oncoming rear of our miracle van. I see him extend his arms in brace position. I think "My hero! He will stop it from hitting them all."

The thought is stifled by the sharp, dull thud of the impact. Jason is dead, I think. His head is surely crushed. The van is now resting against the side door of my friend's car. Selwyn is sandwiched between the two. I come awake still enshrouded in the nightmare.

That's when I ran to the van. I got in. I put it in drive and I willed it back into the carport. When I got out, Selwyn was lying on the ground. My friends' car was now further up the driveway. A sound reached my ear. It was Selwyn's strangely calm shout of "Diane! My hands are mangled!"

We would later laugh at his perfect English in the midst of his trauma. We teased him that he was no real Jamaican. His British birth had taken over. Those jokes came way later. At that point there was no room for laughter. Just hot tears.

Jason stood over his dad telling him to get up. "How is Jason not dead?!" I thought. I ran to where Selwyn lay. He looked up at me in obvious pain. The broken bones were visible, gaping through ripped flesh, as some fingers on his extended, contorted hands hung crooked and limp.

Our friends snapped into action. They are former army officers. In addition to that fact, just the week before, they had needed to call an ambulance for a family member. They had the number at their fingertips. In no time plans were made to rush Selwyn to the ER while Denise and our sitter would stay with the children.

As I ricocheted between tears and adrenaline overdose, two voices brought me back to sanity. The first was Jason's telling me to change that face since he didn't like to see my face like that. The other was Tal's telling me that if I didn't stop crying, I would not be allowed to accompany Selwyn in the ambulance, which by now was quickly but carefully pulling into the driveway where Selwyn still lay on the ground.

I learned from Tal and Denise that before Selwyn tried to stop the van, he had deftly moved Jason out of the way. Selwyn still has no recollection of having done that. Such is the instinct of a father. My only instinct was to keep the hero-dad alive.

Since there was no way I was allowing Selwyn out of my sight, I quickly pulled myself together and took to making sure Selwyn stayed awake, as we raced to the hospital. The ambulance service was excellent, and as we learned from our frequent use in the months that followed, we couldn't have asked for better.

That said, the relatively short journey seemed like an eternity. Even though the sirens were blaring, the ambulance seemed to slowly pick its way through the night traffic. Or at least so it seemed to me. For some reason the things that still linger in my mind are the heart stopping awareness that our roads were so bumpy and pothole ridden and the strobe-like glare of the lights of the other vehicles on the road. Despite that, being on the inside of the ambulance was surreally peaceful. My only job was to hold on to my loved one's arm and will him to stay awake. I was taking that job very seriously.

43

Doctor Doctor

Now, I did say this was the best-planned accident, didn't I? Well, let's just see how I came to that conclusion.

As soon as we arrive at the hospital, the medical staff rushes into action. In no time Selwyn is on a table in the ER and his clothes (nice and new I might add... Funny the things that stand out) are being unceremoniously cut away from his body.

Strangely enough my mind flits to the fact that in addition to mangled hands, shredded clothes, and damaged vehicles, there was another "fatality" in the accident. It was the brand-new pair of glasses that Selwyn had just picked up that day and had been holding in his hand. Peculiar the things that bounce around in a traumatized brain.

Anyway, decisions were happening really quickly. Selwyn's pelvis had split completely open on the left side. I shuddered as someone commented that, had he not fallen, Selwyn's femur could have pushed right up into his abdomen. My stomach was now chock full of butterflies.

I was always happy that Selwyn gave me butterflies. But, in truth, this time these were not the lovely kind. These were violent butterflies angrily jostling each other. I wanted them gone. I wanted them gone so very badly.

In the blink of an eye, Selwyn was rushed away from me and into surgery. I, in turn, stumbled from the emergency room and into the surge of family and friends who had quickly gathered on hearing the news. Stunned and stupefied by grief, the tears again quickly came. I tried to explain what had happened, but was doing a miserable job of it.

Thankfully, I was eventually whisked away to a quiet corner of the hospital by a dear, long-standing friend of ours, to await the end of the endless surgery. She would accompany me to the recovery room, when they finally announced the end of the surgery. My friend was a medical student at that very hospital. By the way, did I mention that she was also an acclaimed actor? Hold on to that little tidbit, because it would become extremely important—life and death important.

So, my friend, the medical student, morphed into my friend the actor. Respectful of hospital protocol, she distanced herself from me, referring to me as "Mrs. Batchelor" and her dear friend, my husband on the recovery bed, as "the patient." With that, we hovered over Selwyn's bed, as our friend asked all the student-doctor questions of the patient who, to my great relief, was now beginning to respond.

Selwyn's eyes fluttered open. Then to my horror they became saucer wide. He lurched upward and then fell back onto the bed, his eyes rolling to the back of his head. He became totally unresponsive to our calling his name.

Panicked, I motioned frantically for the nurses to come over and solve the problem. They were strangely unmoved. I quickly made a call to my brother-in-law, the celebrated Dr. Cecil Batchelor. He was also unruffled. He said something about trusting the medical staff. After all, he expected them to be extra careful knowing the patient was his brother.

Maybe I did not possess the vocabulary to properly explain myself at that point. I became hysterical. They responded by kicking me out of the recovery room. I was desperate. I cried to GOD, the only one really listening to me. And HE listened. Big time!

I found myself outside, having been unceremoniously ejected from the recovery room. My friend was left inside, since it just happened that in that phase of her medical studies, at that very point, she needed to log some hours in the recovery room.

So, my med-student-actor friend, herself quite concerned for her friend lying unconscious on the recovery bed, meekly approached the seemingly unconcerned nurses. "Excuse me!" she said in her most respectful med-student voice. "I notice the patient over there is exhibiting such and such symptoms, yet you both seem unconcerned. Tell me please, what am I missing?"

It is at this point that the staff suddenly snapped into action. They made a quick call to the lead surgeon, who hurriedly instructed them on what to do to revive said patient—the love of my life, the father of my three young children, and a dear friend to the med-student herself.

As it turned out, Selwyn was strongly allergic to one of the anesthesia drugs. Had my friend not been there, had she not intervened, Selwyn would not have surfaced. He could have died on the recovery bed!

Did I mention that our friend had to face the mean time of a dream deferred—her long-held dream of becoming a medical doctor? Well, all of us, her friends, were nonplussed, gob smacked, and downright shocked, when she was not accepted into the Medical Faculty, while we were students at the same university. She was the indisputable brains of our outfit. She was a natural-born student, and added to that she had worked really hard. How could it be? Simple answer? Sovereign GOD!

You see, what none of us knew then, was that she had in fact been accepted to study medicine the year she had applied, but owing to an administrative snafu, she never received the acceptance letter. That there had ever been such a letter only became known when, years later, by then almost at the end of completing her masters, she stumbled across the letter, as she was helping a professor sort through some papers.

The professor admitted to having found the letter long after my friend had moved on to further studies and thought it best to leave things as they were. Our friend had changed course and pursued studies toward a doctorate instead of an M.D., eventually completing her Ph.D.

Many years later, she had finally decided to follow her long-held dream of becoming a medical doctor.

Our friend had to face the mean time, of a dream deferred. In the meantime, GOD was working a purpose greater than we could have imagined. So, whatever caused the administrative bungle that blocked my friend's early entrance to the field of medicine, was no accident. Just when my husband, her friend, lay dying in the recovery room, her presence there made a life-or-death difference. Meet Sovereign GOD, WHO works all things together for the good of those that love HIM!

"And we know [with great confidence] that God [who is deeply concerned about us] causes all things to work together [as a plan] for good for those who love God, to those who are called according to His plan and purpose" (Romans 8:28, AMP).

44

Blessed Assurance

N ow that by itself would be enough to marvel at how well planned this accident was, but there's more! The accident occurred in the February of 2003. Selwyn had not long before become aware of a very prestigious international health insurance provider. He was excited about them because of their renowned reputation for excellent customer care. This level of VIP service, however, came at a commensurate cost. That meant that the products were out of our reach. After all, Selwyn was trying to handle providing for his young family on only one income. After much prayer and contemplation, however, he finally bit the bullet.

Selwyn bought the health insurance policy in December. The accident occurred the following February! Two weeks after that, Selwyn's colon ruptured. Within minutes of being rushed to the hospital with stomach pains and a fever, he was on the operating table. This time they knew not to apply the same dosage of anesthesia. But he came out of surgery wearing a colostomy bag, which he had to use for 3 months. His health teetered back and forth owing to numerous infections.

Because of the excellent insurance plan, we were able to afford the nurses for home care and two excellent therapists, who literally got him out of bed and on his feet again. By August of that same year, he was able to again walk unaided.

No one but GOD could have foreseen the grave need we would have for the excellent care and attention that was the benefit of the health insurance plan. What a joy it was to be able to decline the many offers of help to cover our medical bills, because everything was securely taken care of by direct payment to the service providers!

What a relief it was to have expert doctors confer with our local doctors confirming their treatment options. The insurance company declared that our Jamaican doctors were doing an excellent job. They also assured them and me of their willingness to airlift Selwyn to other treatment facilities, if the need should ever arise. That brought a lot of peace of mind.

Our GOD had gone before us to make the rough places smooth. HE was, is, and continues to be our best insurance against the vicissitudes of life. HE is our Blessed Assurance.

45

Lucy

Now here's another story I must tell. This one concerns the "offending" vehicle—the one that nearly took my husband and son's lives.

You may recall that we started life as two struggling high-school teachers. At that time, we walked, rode the buses or, when we could afford it, hired taxis to transport us wherever we needed to go. Eventually, as our jobs changed, we became the owners of a few cars finally landing on a lovely Toyota Camry as our designated family car.

We tried to be mindful of others who were not as fortunate to have their own vehicle, so we offered rides, whenever it was convenient. As a couple with a sedan, that arrangement worked perfectly. We always had space for at least three others.

When Jonathan came, and added a car seat, we could still offer rides. Even when Jason arrived 20 months later, we could still accommodate a passenger in the car along with our growing family. When our daughter, Jovanna, graced us with her presence, however, all that changed. We could barely find room for the three car seats that took up all of the rear seats. That was when I began to yearn for a real family car.

You may recall that my heart's desire had always been to be a mother and stay at home to raise my family. Being quite the daydreamer, I had always pictured myself in a station wagon. I guess that must have been the epitome of a family car in my day.

Though my father had possessed large cars like a Buick, a Rambler Rebel, and more than one family-sized Mercedes Benz, I still felt that our family of five siblings would have been way better served by owning a station wagon, when we took the many cross-island road trips. I won't even go into my father's habit of piling in more people into our already crowded cars! Let's just say, I still have vivid memories of 13 of us once piled into a VW bug. Only five of us were children. The rest were grown adults! So, when I dreamed of traveling with my family, a station wagon was the car I drove.

During the many years that passed before our children came, I began to notice the efficiency of a family van. They were excellent at packing in people and all their "korouchiz" (a colorful Jamaican word meaning all their attendant stuff). With that, my dream changed. I would get a family van instead. As the years rolled on, the make and model adjusted depending on the size of our faith and the depth of our pockets. We started out dreaming of a Kia Carnival, then we considered a few others, finally settling on a Toyota Noah. Driving through Kingston's narrow, crowded streets became a rubbernecking adventure for me, as I scanned all the passing family vans, mentally totting up their suitability to our growing family.

I need to inform you at this point, that I have a reputation for being quite unaware of cars and their make or model. Selwyn, on the other hand, is a repository of information on cars and on the minute changes that car manufacturers make from year to year to entice trend followers to relinquish perfectly good vehicles in an attempt to be current. This is why you won't find it strange;

that I turned to him to help me decipher a rather strange dream I had one night.

I dreamt that some friends were helping me move quite a bit of stuff out of a house. The stuff seemed to be all mine. When my friends asked where they should put the things, I motioned to a vehicle parked in the yard, and said "Put them in Lucy." Now as dreams go, I cannot recall having actually seen the vehicle in question. I just, somehow, awoke with a sense that the Lucy to which I referred was a spacious van.

So, I turned to my resident car expert to find out if he had any idea of a vehicle that could have the name Lucy. He was actually stumped, but after some consideration, he came up with a Lucinda (which was a pretty small car), and a Lucida—a beautiful, luxury, family van.

As we asked around, we discovered that some friends of ours were owners of this special vehicle, so we asked if we could visit to have a look at it. When they graciously complied, it confirmed our first impression. It was an amazingly suitable family van, but it was way too expensive for us to own.

With that, we returned to our search for a Toyota Noah. Now here's another piece of information that would help in the telling of this tale: In Jamaica we are right by driving on the left (humor me).

That means that, since in Japan they also drive on the left, we are beneficiaries of the Japanese car market that usually sends us very gently-used cars with innovative features that don't get included in their cars made for the general export market.

As I surveyed the vans on our roads, I also made sure to keep abreast of the ones that sat on the many used car lots around the city. One particular Toyota Noah grabbed our attention. Maybe that was because of its peculiar mint green color with green tinted windows. At first, we were put off by the color, but having driven by it regularly, as we traversed Constant Spring Road, we finally decided to go inside the lot to have a closer look.

The car was an emerald gem. It had so many features that appealed to us that, in no time; we had also embraced its unusual color. I was soon sold on the car, but Selwyn decided to do the sensible thing and bring along another car enthusiast to also weigh in on the wisdom of the purchase. This friend was James Loewen, our Mennonite missionary friend who lived in and taught at the Jamaica Theological Seminary opposite our apartment. His family and ours had become fast friends.

Having seen the car, James too agreed that it would be a good buy for our family. With that Selwyn assured the salesmen that he wished to purchase it and would be back after making the financial arrangements. I was very excited. I had test driven it and was impressed by its spaciousness and ingenious features. We were sure this van, that had been many weeks on the lot, had been waiting there for us.

What a shock it was the next day when Selwyn arrived at the lot to finalize the purchase. The van was not there! The dumbfounded salesmen exclaimed that they had had no traction on the van, till just after Selwyn had left the day before. A group of men arrived shortly afterwards, offered cash for the vehicle, and drove it out of the lot for good. We were terribly disappointed, but we couldn't ignore the way things had unfolded. It was as if the LORD was making sure we would not purchase that van.

That is when we decided to increase our faith to see if there was any possibility, we could indeed purchase the unattainable Toyota Lucida. Selwyn decided to drive to various car lots in search of the van. He found none. In truth, it seemed that our dear friends were the only people on the island who owned that make and model van.

Finally, he recalled that a brother from our church was a car dealer. We drove to his office to find out if he had any information regarding this particular vehicle. As soon as Selwyn mentioned the name, our brother surprised us by remarking that he had in fact never imported that make or model before, but that just that very afternoon, his buyers in Japan had purchased one that should be arriving in his next shipment of cars.

With that he motioned to his computer screen where we saw the most beautiful, pearl white, double-sun-roofed, tastefully detailed Toyota family van. We were able to see the many permutations of its interior and were amazed at its flexible seating arrangements and its suitability for all our young family's needs. The Noah's features paled in comparison. Emblazoned on the side of this dream van were the bold letters LUCIDA. We were trembling with nervous excitement. Did GOD really plan for this beauty of a van to be ours?

As we feared, the price was quite a bit above what we were able to afford, but we decided to step out in faith and ask our brother to reserve it for us. We prayed that during the time it would take to get to Jamaica from Japan and be released through the customs processing, we might somehow find a way to purchase it.

With that, Selwyn began his investigations with the lending agencies and finally landed on an easy loan through our credit union. Our brother, the dealer, had given us an estimated time when the car should be on the lot. The problem was, it would take time to have the loan go through the approval processes. We worried that the lengthy approval process could mean the car would arrive before we had the money in hand.

When the time came for the car to arrive, the loan was still being processed. Selwyn with trepidation approached the dealer. As soon as he saw Selwyn he exclaimed, "You're here about your van, right?"

"Yes", Selwyn timidly responded.

"Well, I know this van is really meant for you," he said in an awed voice.

"Right now, as we speak, I have two shiploads of cars burning off the coast of Japan."

His voice quivered with emotion. "Your van should have been among them."

"Somehow, your van was accidentally left on the dock!" he exclaimed. "This car is definitely meant to be yours!" he finally whooped with emotion, his arms wildly pumping the air.

We left his office in stunned bewilderment. Could GOD really be working in the meantime to give us time to secure the loan? Well, that is exactly what HE did. By the time the car arrived on the island, our loan had been secured, and we joyfully claimed our prize, the car GOD had handpicked for us.

And that is why, when a few months later, Selwyn was crushed by the same van, we did not for one minute entertain the suggestion that our car was cursed and should be sold, as some folks suggested. We knew this was a precious gift, and a sign of GOD's faithful love to us.

Selwyn recovered well and happily drove Lucy on many family trips where we, along with family and friends, comfortably reclined and enjoyed all the ingenious family features provided by our precious Lucida. We would not allow an accident to cause us to doubt GOD's love so pointedly expressed to us in a family van.

46

One Body

The mean time of Selwyn's accident was one that brought me face to face with one of the greatest joys of my life. I became keenly aware of being carried by the love, prayers, and practical help of the BODY of CHRIST. I can't name all the ones who became the physical body of CHRIST to me.

But I will tell of my friend who was always too busy to pay me a visit when things were going well, yet would arrive at my home every morning after the accident happened, so she could help me get my children ready and take them to school. Both her children were by then grown adults.

I will tell of my single friend who chartered a taxicab at midnight to stand in the hallway, after one of Selwyn's surgeries, just to give me a bear hug and say, "I love you, and I am praying for you" before immediately turning around and heading back into the dark night.

I will tell of the couple that offered to keep the children while I waited outside Selwyn's operating theatre, and the husband who spent a sleepless night trying to console my inconsolable baby girl, just so I could spend the night sleeping near Selwyn in the hospital recliner.

I will tell of the young mom who, after heading home from a full day of work, then dealing with her own children, came by in the night to help me sort through business documents to ensure that Selwyn's business continued while he was in hospital.

I will tell of my friend who helped me learn to change a colostomy bag, when Selwyn no longer had nursing care.

I will tell of those who cooked meals, those who prayed, those who called, those who were GOD with skin on to me.

It's funny now to recall some of the ways the Body showed us love. Our church seemed frustrated that eventually the only real help we needed was prayer. They sent a member of their prayer team to regularly pray with us, as we faced the various medical challenges. Still not satisfied that they had done enough, one day the pastor in charge of member care announced that a sister from the church was being sent to our home to help in whatever way we needed. Such were the ways in which we were carried by the Church of JESUS CHRIST.

I would not trade the chance to experience this depth of community for the world. After all, this is what it's all about. John 13:35 (AMP) says it so clearly, "By this everyone will know that you are My disciples, if you have love and unselfish concern for one another."

I love seeing the Body of Christ in full, active love mode! And it is even more special if you get to be the recipient of that love when you are in a time of desperate need. Little did I know that I was about to again have that anguished yet blissful experience some years later. This time, I was to be the patient.

PART FIVE

47

Chasing a Dream Country

SO, I told you that my major at university was Spanish. (Now it's out. Panama family, please forgive my myriad mistakes). Being somewhat of a reluctant scholar, I did not readily seek after study for study's sake. My parents had made it clear that we all had to pursue tertiary studies, so I reasoned that, for me, language was the best option. I had settled on that, since I thought that communication is the tool most needed in spreading the gospel, so knowledge of more than one language would be an asset in that endeavor.

By now you know that especially in our very early years as a couple, the LORD spoke to us quite a bit, and in various ways. One of those ways was through dreams. One night during our very first year of marriage, we both had significant dreams.

They were impactful enough that we both spoke about them the next morning, as soon as we awoke. As we each described our dream, we realized that we had been dreaming of the same place. We had been somewhere in South/Central America we thought, and what stood out to me were the tribal peoples.

Having studied Linguistics, I began to imagine that I might have been receiving a call to Bible translation among a people group without the Bible. Somehow, without the internet, nor any Bible translating organization in Jamaica, I managed to get a hold of, and fill out, an application to Wycliffe Bible Translators. The rest is a blur. I cannot recall whether or not I did post the application, but somewhere in the busyness of life, I forgot all about that desire.

After the children came, and we looked back over our life together, we began to recall the things we believed GOD had spoken to us. Soon we noticed that everything we thought that HE had said to us had been fulfilled except for one. That one had to do with our dream of being in South/Central America.

We had by then understood that GOD's timing and ways were different from ours. After all, had HE not fulfilled the vision given during the second week of our marriage ten years later? Hadn't the children begun to come 14 years after the promise? We decided to be on the lookout to see how GOD would fulfill this dream. For by then, we had come to understand that when we decide to put GOD in a box, HE always stands on the outside with a bemused look on HIS face and then proceeds to blow our minds with HIS "unboxability" and HIS "unfathomableness."

It was then that we made an observation. Selwyn had been regularly attending annual business conferences. Most of the attendees at these conferences were Spanish speakers who hailed from nearly every South/Central American country. Maybe we had been too literal in our interpretation of our dreams. Maybe GOD would use us to touch these people via our conference interactions.

Well, there was indeed a conference involved in the fulfillment of these dreams, but not in the way either of us would have imagined.

48

Many Years...

The year was 2005, our family had spent the previous Christmas in the bitter Winnipeg cold with our dear friends, Marci and James Loewen and their three children, our children's first childhood friends, Joshua, Sarah, and Micah. Micah, we dubbed Ja-Micah, since he was the one born in Jamaica and shockingly even had a birthmark in the shape of the island.

The warm fellowship we all enjoyed with them was almost enough to make us forget we were freezing unbearably. No fault of theirs, the weather that winter was the coldest they had experienced in 50 years!

Sometime near the end of our lovely visit, they made a proposal. They told us they were planning to move to Vancouver and would love us to consider moving there also. They promised to give us all the help we would need to get settled. They also suggested we could buy land together and build just far enough apart to still remain good friends. That last part they added with a mischievous chuckle.

When they lived in Jamaica, James had never stopped greeting my numerous phone calls to Marci with an exaggerated mock exasperation. "You again!" The fact is that, being great friends as well as co-founders of the family support group Hibiscus MOM's, we had a lot to say to each other (so take that, James!)

Now you need to know that my business trip to Norway was just the first of many. My job had evolved to entail quite a bit of travel. My most striking observation coming home from each new country had been how exquisitely lovely was my own island home. I developed a renewed appreciation for our little rock in the sea. Nowhere else could compare. That is until I was landing in Vancouver BC.

Although I had been forewarned, I was totally unprepared for the amazing juxtaposition of mountain and seafront framed by a blazing sunset that greeted me the very first time my plane was landing there. I was completely blown away by its beauty! Finally, a place as lovely as my island.

Having visited a few more times, I soon fell in love with its many views, its melee of cultures, and its modern yet old-fashioned charm. I then declared that, should I ever decide to make my home away from my precious Jamaica, for sure that home would be in Vancouver.

As a matter of fact, our friendship with the Loewens had begun when, on learning they were Canadians, I had blurted out how much I loved Vancouver. It was then that I had learnt that Marci was herself from Vancouver. Of course, we would become fast friends.

I had harbored a desire for my children to experience living for a few years in a society where things were more orderly and structured than in Jamaica. I also wanted them to learn another language. I thought that would be crucial to expanding their view of the world. Here was my opportunity. In Canada I could immerse them in the French language.

Why then was I needing to draw upon every ounce of the good manners I had learnt from my mother in order to respond with gratitude when my friends, the Loewens, made their offer? I didn't recognize myself. I should have been ecstatic. I was puzzled.

Not to look the proverbial gift horse in the mouth, we decided to begin the process of applying to migrate to Canada. I couldn't shake the complete lack of enthusiasm that morphed into outright annoyance at all the questions I needed to answer in order to complete the application forms.

It was during this time that I stumbled upon an MSN online article. Its title was "Panama—a Haven for Retirees." At the time retirement for both of us was many years away, but something inside me stirred wildly. What was this?

As I read the article, I became more and more intrigued with this country that had failed to make an impression on me when I had visited some time before. When Selwyn came home from work that day, I showed him the article. He, the language-challenged, science major, also became excited about this Spanish-speaking country. To quote the rabbit in Alice in Wonderland, "Curiouser and curiouser!"

What was even more curious was the fact that we had already planned to attend another conference in Panama that November, only a month or so away. With that, I began my investigations into this country with which I had bizarrely begun to be obsessed.

Interestingly at the same time I was doing my research into life in Panama, another online article surfaced listing Vancouver as the happiest city in the world. I still was strangely unmoved. It could have been because at this time, we again began to recall our coinciding dreams during our early marriage—the ones where we were in a Central/South American country. Could this be that?

The first firm test was a call to the appropriate Panamanian authorities to see if Selwyn could continue his business there. After a few rings we were connected with the office. We managed to find someone who not only spoke to us in English, but also promised to forward to us a copy of the business regulations (IN ENGLISH). When it arrived by email not long afterwards, it specified that it was totally possible for Selwyn to continue his business there.

The curious thing was that we had not long before purchased a home, which I had been certain was meant to be our forever home. The idea of leaving it had not been a thought I entertained. As a matter of fact, I recall the day one of my friends, a Panamanian woman married to a Jamaican man, came by for a visit.

As we sat on the edge of my bed, she disclosed that after more than 30 years of making Jamaica her home, she was feeling the call to return to Panama. She explained that it would not be long before she left, as they had both prayed about it and were sure that is what they should do. She had even remarked that she believed GOD would be calling others from Jamaica to go too. I remember telling her how much I would miss them, as Mixela and her husband Tyrone were beloved members of our church community. Cue her shock, when it was I who was now expressing interest in moving there.

By the time November rolled around, I had found a small Panamanian-American school that was using the same curriculum our children were using in their Jamaican "homeschool." (Our boys were being taught by a friend who had enrolled about ten children of varying ages in classes at her home). In finding the school in Panama, we also found what seemed to be a very suitable church.

Through another Panamanian connection (a former student from the Language Training Centre and also a member of our church), I was given a whole swathe of brochures from a Panamanian housing expo held a few months before. In no time, through a series of "GOD-incidences", we had found potential homes, school and church. And we hadn't even gone there yet!

49

...And 5 Days

Whaen we finally arrived in Panama for the conference, we were armed with all the school certification and information required to enroll our children into school there. We also had in hand a few reference letters to a reputable bank from our dear Panamanian friend. And we had recommendations of communities in which to search for a suitable rented home, while we took the time to decide where to settle.

That in itself is a story to tell, because even though I had seen and fallen in love with a beautiful community featured in one of the housing brochures, Selwyn had strongly warned me that, under no circumstance, should I set my mind on buying so quickly. He cautioned that we would need at least a year to make a proper assessment of the best place to settle our family. Grudgingly, I submitted to his wisdom. It was the wise thing to do.

Our conference lasted two days. Naïvely, I had expected to be able to do all my reconnaissance and migration preparation in three days, so we booked to be there only an extra three days. As a friend of mine used to quip, "Fools and children, GOD protects." That was surely the case with us.

On the morning of the last day of the conference, we decided to capitalize on our hotel's being in the banking district, and we walked to the nearby bank our friend had recommended. We met with the client services officer, who invited us into her office. No sooner had we presented our documents with a view to opening our account than the phone on her desk rang. She excused herself to answer it, and spoke for a few minutes before returning to our conversation with a breathy "So, as we were saying about your mortgage..." We politely corrected her.

As I mentioned before, our goal was to find a suitable place to rent, so even though I had my eye on a few places, they were off the table. My husband had wisely warned me against making a rash home purchase. After all, we really did not know the country.

The agent apologized, and returned to perusing the papers we had presented. Not many minutes later, the same thing happened again. The phone interrupts her, she rejoins us with a question about a mortgage, I correct her.

By the time this had happened the third time, I said, "It seems like you would really love to tell us about your mortgage program here. How about you tell us what it would look like, should we wish to buy a house, say for...?" and at this point I slyly inserted the figure on a townhouse for sale that had also caught my eye.

She seemed pretty eager to run the numbers. When she proffered the paper with the details of the terms and payments, both our eyes widened. The figure I had suggested was significantly higher than the cost of the home we had recently purchased in Jamaica, but the monthly payments exactly matched what we were currently paying there. That was a very pleasant surprise. Mortgage rates were much lower in Panama. Good to know!

I took the papers and stashed them in the folder she had given to us, and seemingly relieved of her burning desire to explain the mortgage process, she finally signed us up. We were now customers of the bank. With that, we departed to embark on the rest of our whirlwind, fact-finding and migration preparation mission.

50

Mi Casa, Su Casa

Before arriving in Panama, I had had the pleasure of speaking to a young woman with the unforgettable name Nedelka Bustamante. This name stood out, because Nedelka in itself was quite unique, but that it was paired with the surname Bustamante took it to a whole other level. Bustamante was a surname I had only ever heard before as the one a Jamaican national hero had adopted, after he gave up the comparatively run-of-the-mill name Clarke. Nedelka was the only other Bustamante I knew of. I was looking forward to meeting her at the school appointment we had set up.

As charming in person as she was on the phone, Nedelka greeted us warmly, took the papers we had brought, and introduced us to the principal. Although we were at first stunned by the small size and awkward layout of the school, we were soon captivated by the warmth of everyone we met.

The words of the then principal, Dr Martens, still warm my heart when I recall them. As we were leaving his office, he reached for a school yearbook, handed it to us, and said, "Take this for your children, so they will see who their new friends will be."

Before we left the compound, Nedelka again reminded me of the name of the neighborhood she had suggested during our phone conversations prior to our arriving in the country. I was looking forward to more interaction between our family and this gentle woman.

The neighborhood she had suggested was located in the former Canal Zone. It was in fact a former army barracks, and seemed quite old. Nevertheless, not to ignore the wise advice of a local, we decided to check it out. And we were glad we did. We eventually found a lovely apartment to rent in Clayton. As a matter of fact, we later saw that Nedelka's suggestion had GOD's handprint all over it.

Thanks to my Panamanian-Jamaican friend Mixela, we had been picked up from the hotel and were being escorted around by her sister-in-law, an interior decorator, and her sister, a lawyer. This combination soon proved very pivotal to the success of our three-day reconnaissance mission.

As we were on our way to the school, we drove by a gated community with its name inscribed on the perimeter wall that formed its border. It seemed to spark a memory. Why was that name so familiar? As we drove closer to the gate and could see inside, the reason became clear. This was the same community I had spent so many hours researching from my computer back home! There it was with its beautiful homes and tall, majestic, forest trees.

But my husband had forbidden me from considering a purchase, so... Truth is, we were very used to window-shopping new homes and communities, so I was itching just to take a look. I was very pleased when it was Selwyn who said, "We have time. Let's go look at them." Nice! I could drool over these homes up close. Soon we had gone through the security gates, entered the sales office, and were seated opposite the sales manager.

The most remarkable thing had happened when we opened our car door to step into the fresh, warm breeze.

The sound of birdcall almost drowned out our voices. No way was this real! Did they install a sound track to make the neighborhood more appealing? As we stared up into the giant trees that dwarfed the houses, the many birds that flitted among the branches answered our question. This was gloriously real.

The sales manager also happened to be an architect and coincidentally had Jamaican roots! Additionally, his family was the developer, and they also all had settled their own families in homes within the project. I was enthralled, as he showed us the architectural model of the community. I was even more impressed by our visit to the model homes. This was something to aspire after.

But Selwyn was right. We needed to take the time to study the city and its neighborhoods, before we could settle on the one most suitable for our family. The only thing we knew so far was that it was within the price range of our current mortgage payment, and that it was less than half an hour away from the school in which we had enrolled our children.

Having circuited the community, we returned to the sales office. What happened next left me with my mouth wide open. After hearing that only a few lots remained unpurchased, and that with a relatively small deposit, one could reserve one, Selwyn suddenly whipped out the checkbook he was carrying. Deftly he filled in the required sum, ripped the page from the book, and handed it to the salesman. I was at a loss for words.

When my words finally found me, I used them to stutter in a whisper, "Didn't you say we were going to wait?" At that he calmly reassured me that he had thought it through. Taking me aside he reminded me of the mortgage document we still had in our possession. He pointed out that during the conversation regarding the price, it had dawned on him that the monthly payment was not outside of our reach. He was impressed to take a leap of faith, so he did. I was leaping right beside him.

Soon the lawyer who accompanied us was reviewing the agreement and terms. I thought I must have been in a dream. We were so much closer to owning the home I had only been able to dream of. The real miracle though, was that, when we returned to settle in Panama less than two months later, all the lots had not only been sold, but the price had appreciated so much, that there was no way we would have been able to afford it, had we waited. Look at GOD!

Our three extra days in Panama after our conference saw us with:

A bank account opened,

The boys registered in school,

A church identified,

A reservation made on a forever home,

An interim rental lease signed, and

Basic furniture bought.

It was the most accomplished three days we had ever spent. GOD had given us both the same dream and HE was hastening to fulfill it.

"And as regards the double repetition of the dream to Pharaoh, it is that the thing is established by God and God will hasten to do it" (Genesis 41:32).

51

A Dream Realized

When we returned with our family early the following January, it was with a strong sense of being right where we were meant to be. And remember how I had thought maybe I'd be translating the Bible for an indigenous group in a Spanish-speaking country? Well, guess what?

The pastor of our new church and his family had lived for years among one of Panama's seven indigenous peoples. They had translated the Bible into the language of that group. In fact, the church had been one of the organizations involved in translating the Bible into every indigenous language in Panama. And the thing that blew us away was that the pastor of our church was the one overseeing Bible translation projects within the whole region. The organization he represented? Wycliffe Bible Translators—the very same organization to which I had applied all those years before!

As I got more involved with the church's missions program, I discovered that at the time that I had filled in the application, Wycliffe had not been accepting entrants from the Caribbean.

Selwyn and I spent many a service in those early months just wiping the tears that flowed. As the worship songs seesawed easily between English and Spanish, we were astounded at the GOD whose word never returned to HIM void. There I was in Panama surrounded by all these Bible translators and eventually having a hand in their support through serving on the church's missions coordinating program. Look at God!

And as for interacting with the indigenous people, I have had the privilege of meeting many of the native language translators from among Panama's seven indigenous peoples. I have also had close fellowship with Kuna people both by visiting their pristine, beach-island paradise and by singing alongside them (sometimes in their own language) during our annual Christmas productions. Actually, it was a Christmas production and one of those indigenous peoples, the Kuna, which also helped confirm that GOD had indeed placed us in Panama.

52

Rain Rain

When we arrived in January of 2006, we were nonplussed to see the storefronts all displaying summer sales. Panama was less than two hours away from Jamaica. What happened to the cool Christmas breezes? Well, there were breezes, but not at all cool. And the sun beat down so mercilessly that the grass was baked brown, and the earth was a cracked desertscape.

Honestly, despite all the heat, I still didn't get why they called that season Summer. That is until winter came. Yes. Winter came barging in as soon as Summer was over.

Without so much as a preamble, the cloudless skies became obliterated by the blackest of clouds. The winds whipped through the neighborhood, felling even giant trees. The longest pitchforks of lightning I had ever seen split the darkness, and heralded the thunder of the apocalypse. (I was as glad to draw comfort from my children who scrambled into our bed, as they did from me.)

But it was the rain that did me in. The merciless rain fell like arrows from the skies, before becoming curtains of water that swelled every stream and made lakes out of all the open fields in which my children had frolicked only a few short days before. The rain seemed unending. And somehow, if ever there was a reprieve, it ended just at the time when I would be stuck in the line of traffic snaking through the schoolyard, trying to retrieve children who would inevitably be wet by the time they made it to the car.

After a while, I devised a way to make the dash from the garage to the uncovered steps that led to our second-floor apartment. I would adjust to this weather. After all, our home under construction was supposed to be ready in just a few months. We could do this. "This" was a three-bedroom, one-and-a-half-bathroom apartment. It had been beautifully renovated, and the children enjoyed all the open green spaces that surrounded it.

When we had rented it in November, we had had no idea how soon the weather would change, and more importantly, for how long. That was why we were then not at all fazed by the off-white carpet that ran throughout the apartment. After all, the children would spend most of their time in the many nearby outdoor play spaces that had caused Jonathan to remark, "It looks like children are important here."

And we could go for a year with all the children in one room, while Selwyn made a home-office out of one of the bedrooms. The children were by then, eight, six, and four years old. With some creativity they could share a room.

I had prepared myself to move into our new home in a year, despite the contractor's promise that it would be ready in nine months. I was being generous and sparing myself any disappointment by planning on being in the little apartment for three extra months. Our home would be ready in a year. We could do this in the meantime. (I can hear you chuckling. Are you being mean?)

I didn't bargain on the rain. I could never have imagined months upon months of heavy, interminable rain showers. Soon I had to throw neatness to the wind, and allow my children to play outdoor games including football (the one where you use your foot) in the living room. As the off-white carpet began to show the effects of wet, muddy feet, I purchased a brown overlay rug. It didn't look messy, but it sucked all the light from the room.

My mood began to reflect the darkness. It was becoming a mean time. It also soon became evident that our home under construction was nowhere near ready to be finished in a year. We finally decided it would be better for our whole family, if we sought a more suitable place in which to wait.

An opportunity arose when some fellow parents from the boys' school announced that they would soon be vacating their rental property in our neighborhood. They would be moving to a home they had recently purchased and were almost finished renovating.

As soon as we were certain that they had a moving date secured, we contacted their former landlords and made plans to move into their more suitable apartment. I arranged with the telephone and gas companies to have our accounts transferred to the new building, and I contracted a moving company.

Selwyn and I began to have some unease about our decision the week before we were to move. As we prayed for guidance the LORD led me to a passage I had not noticed before. It was Jeremiah 38:15, and this was what leapt off the page: "Even if I did give you counsel, you would not listen to me." I was astonished. As I read further, I saw that though the prophet eventually gave advice to the king, he did not accept it, even after promising to obey. The king and his people in turn suffered a grave consequence. I decided, before the LORD, that I would do whatever HE said. It instantly became clear. HE wanted us to stay.

With that we cancelled the utility transfers, and called off the moving company. Before we had the opportunity to let our friends know we would not be taking their old rental, they came to advise us that there had been a setback, and they would not be moving in the timeframe they had expected. Even though this confirmed what we believed to be the voice of the LORD, in the meantime, I was miserable.

Some mornings, after dropping the children to school, I would drive up the hill to knock on the pastor's door. His sweet wife, Mary, would welcome me in and not blink an eye when I told her I had come (unannounced) to her home just to sit with her at her piano and harmonize, while she sang and played. Coming from a Caribbean culture, people dropping in was the norm. I later learned that those kinds of impromptu visits were frowned upon. In our American-led church, the norm was to call and make an appointment. Even so, Mary made me feel welcome, and soothed my soul with her gift of music.

I would some evenings escape to my new friend, Judy Gunn's home, just so I could sit in an ordered, light-filled room and hear myself think. She would oblige by hardly speaking. Judy, unlike her sister-in-law Mary, had warned me against visiting her in the morning. She would often be up late working on literacy material for the people group among whom they ministered, so she needed her morning rest.

I believe it was Judy who invited me to join the annual Christmas production. That was how I learned that at our new church, Christmas began in August with rehearsals for a major year-end production. I was happy to have a musical outlet, and even more excited that our whole family except Jovanna (my, by then five-year old) could participate. She would eventually have that joy.

What's more, the choir consisted of people from many different churches who, directed by a very skilled musician, would rehearse weekly till near Christmas, when singers, dancers, and dramatists would come together to present a Christmas spectacular rivaling any Broadway production. Don Jordan, was a picture of grace under pressure, skillfully eliciting beautiful music from our motley group, some of whom honestly shouldn't even sing in the shower.

It was at those rehearsals that I met people from the province of Colon and finally grasped the meaning of our Jamaican folk song, "One two three four, Colon man a come." Most of these people seemed to have a Jamaican connection. As I asked the tall, strapping tenor from Colon if he too had Jamaican heritage, he said no. But, he added, his church had just received a new pastor sent by the Jamaica Baptist Union. Her name was Marvia Lawes, and she had not long arrived in the country.

There was something familiar about the name, but I couldn't recall any Jamaican pastor by that name. By then I had lived more than seven months in Panama, so I felt I was in a position to help her navigate her new country. With that in mind, I gave Alejandro my number, and asked him to pass it on to his new pastor. When next I saw him, he confirmed that he had done it.

As I had not yet received a call, I asked him to share her number with me, so I could call her. When I did, no one answered. I left her a message explaining that, although she didn't know me, I was Jamaican too and wanted to meet her. Some days later my phone rang. When I answered, the woman on the line said, "Hello, this is Marvia Lawes.'

I quickly recognized the name and hastened to explain why I had left her a message. Before I could go very far, she interrupted. "Diane Batchelor, I know you, and have been trying to find you since I got here." I was perplexed. As it turned out, we had frequently interacted during my days in the shipping industry. In the almost nine years since I had resigned, she had answered the call to ministry, had retrained, and was now the pastor of the First Isthmian Baptist Church in Colon. A mutual friend in Jamaica had given her my number. I was excited to be able to renew our contact.

When I told her where I lived, she remarked that she frequently stayed in the same neighborhood at the home of one of her deacons. Soon, we were planning a rendez-vous for the next time she would be in the city. When the day came, she took the short walk from where she was staying to our small apartment.

As we ate and talked, she mentioned that her church encompassed English, Spanish, and Kuna members. Selwyn was quick to tell her of our church's involvement in Bible translation, and offered to gift her church some

256

Bibles in the Kuna language. At the end of the visit, as it was not yet raining, we decided to walk with her to the home nearby, so we would know where to deliver the Bibles.

We were pleasantly surprised to note that her deacon's home was the very one we had often admired on our evening family strolls during the dry season. Many of Clayton's former Canal Zone barrack homes had been purchased by Panamanians and refurbished into beautiful family residences. The one in which she was a guest stood out among them. We had often wished to be able to see inside.

A few weeks later, a rare sunny day, we piled our children into our car along with their toys and a box of Kuna Bibles. We had taken to driving to the beautiful playground in our prospective neighborhood, so our children could play safely, while we inspected the construction site to gauge the progress. We promised the children that we would be heading directly to the playground, only stopping to drop off the promised Bibles.

True to our word we sat in our car, as the deacon came out to meet us to collect the box. In an instant, before we could even open our car trunk, the heavens opened and such a downpour began that the deacon had to retreat to the safety of his covered two-car garage. From its protection, he motioned to us to park our car there while he collected the Bibles.

One glance at the skies told us what we feared. There would be no playing outdoors that day. As we ruefully explained the situation to the children, the deacon invited us in. We were happy to accept. We had always been curious about his beautiful home. Inside, we met his gracious wife, Yolanda, who offered us refreshments.

As we seated ourselves in their lovely home, the children became open in their curiosity. Equally curious, but more practiced at restraint, we instructed the children to remain seated. Arcelio Hartley, the deacon, then turned to them and asked if they wished to look around. They sprang up from their seats with a "yes", and we were happy to join the tour.

This is when we realized that the home was really four apartments, two of which had been modified into one two-story home. The other two were still separate, but a skillful facade had given the appearance of one complete home. From our tour we discovered that all of one side of the lovely home was unoccupied. There was also no carpeting to be seen anywhere.

Arcelio disclosed that he had been using the vacant apartments to host occasional church gatherings. When asked, he explained that they had never been rented, but he was open to renting to the right person. To cut a long story short, we became the right person.

Within weeks we found ourselves as the new renters of not one, but two apartments in a beautiful home with its own covered carport. One of the apartments was semi-furnished, which was perfect for us, since our furniture from Jamaica had not yet arrived in Panama. The thing that most shocked us was that with twice the space plus furnishings, and a covered carport, the rent we were asked to pay was a mere $50 more than we had paid in our previous rented apartment.

The Hartleys quickly became our family in Panama, and to this day we marvel at the way GOD directed us to them through HIS word and through the rain. And, by the way, when December came, and the rains went away, we were very ecstatic to embrace a Panamanian Summer.

So, there you have it. Even when it doesn't seem to make sense, we should trust GOD in the meantime. HIS word does not return to HIM void. It always accomplishes what it was sent to do. I have seen it with my own eyes, and I am in awe!

PART SIX

53

A Father's Lasting Lesson

Those who knew my dad know that he was his very own kind of special. He loved profoundly but wasn't very warm in his expression of it. He was a merciless teaser and instead of warm embraces, he gave bone crushing hugs and playful punches. That said, if he loved you, you knew it. He loved me, and I knew it.

So here comes my birthday. I'm a recently married twenty-something. We meet at the hospital to welcome my sister's newest addition to her family, baby Matthew. I wait for the greeting and the happy birthday. It doesn't come. I'm shocked and hurt.

A few days later it's the weekend, and I'm at my parents' home. My niece and nephew are visiting from the Cayman Islands and, as the designated favorite aunt, I'm there to hang with them for the day.

Not one to hold my feelings in, I take every opportunity I get to let my dad know that he saw me on my birthday and didn't even acknowledge that for me it was a special day. As we pass each other around the home, I poke him sharply and scold, "You! You didn't even wish me a happy birthday!"

He is busy scaling, gutting, and seasoning fish. He is obviously preparing to have one of his famous outdoor fish fry gatherings. Nothing strange here. Both our parents are people magnets and had been dubbed Mummy T and Daddy T by all the young people in their church.

Having tired a bit of scolding, poking, and prodding my dad for his great offence, I notice the children at loose ends, and I offer to take them to the park nearby. My parents are grateful for the offer, and the children happily skip with me to play for a bit in the outdoors.

When they eventually tire, we walk home in time to see some of the usual suspects arriving. As I expected, these are the young folks from the church my parents attend, many of whom are friends I had made while studying at the nearby university.

Suddenly, I see some other friends of mine approaching the gate. They were definitely not among those who were frequent visitors to my parents' home. "What are you guys doing here?" I call out, thrilled to see them, but equally perplexed. By now there is a buzz of people happily chatting and laughing—the usual Daddy T fish fry vibe.

"You mean you don't know yet?" my friend Faith asked incredulously, her eyes ricocheting between my face and the already gathered crowd of family and friends. Aba by her side gave a playful chuckle and continued, "DT, this party is for you! It's for your birthday!"

I was speechless. I had witnessed the entire preparation and execution, had even got myself out of the way, so they could carry out the finishing touches, and I had been clueless the whole time. All this had been for me! My dad had not forgotten my birthday, instead he had been preparing to thoroughly delight and surprise me.

As you may imagine, I was also very embarrassed. I had chided, prodded, poked, and reprimanded my dad for his grave offence the whole time that he was actively putting in place the surprise of my life.

To boot, he had himself picked out a lovely gift for me— a beautiful chunky necklace and a crafty jewelry box in which to store it. The magnitude of this gesture was not lost on me, because my dad was not known to give special-occasion gifts.

As you may imagine, I tried desperately to apologize for my previous remonstrance and mistrust. My dad just smirked and hugged me warmly.

54

Slow Learner?

For many years I suffered from sciatica. Even before the children came, the sciatica had forced me to do away with a stick shift and rely on automatic transmission cars. Kingston's rush hour traffic had often caused me to limp home in great pain. By the time the children came and I had undergone multiple surgeries, adhesions became another source of pain. Finally, a doctor in Panama after examining me, felt that most of the pain I suffered all over my body was more than likely due to fibromyalgia. I had reacted violently to all the classic trigger points.

Because of this, I am forced to be gentle with myself. Strenuous exercise, heavy lifting, and the like are things from which, by necessity I am banned. I was not happy, and I complained frequently to my FATHER. After all, HE made me this way.

Why?

How mean!

Through the years, I kept whining.

Every time I had to take pain medication I whined.

Every time I had to retreat from another attempt at establishing a workout routine, I whined.

Every time I was once again cautioned not to lift, push or pull something heavy, I whined.

When I did it anyway and was rewarded with crippling pain and days of immobility, I whined.

Every time I was hit with what felt like muscle contracts in the abdomen after sudden movement, I whined.

"Why didn't I have my children naturally?"

All these painful adhesions were making my life unbearable.

"Why do I have sciatica?"

"Why do I hurt all over?"

"Why?"

"Why?"

"Why?"

I poked and prodded my FATHER.

I questioned HIS love.

I whined.

Mid-2017, a friend offered to act as my personal trainer. She was newly certified and positive that she would be able to get me into shape without undue pain. I recounted to her the many previous failed attempts I had endured. She was not deterred. I said to her, "Let's do this, but know that every time I start a program, something happens to cause me to stop."

Our first day began well. We moved through a series of routines walking through our hilly neighborhood, utilizing the new exercise equipment in our park, and finally ending up in my family room for cool down exercises. Everything went so well that I was encouraged. We made a plan to do this three times a week, and I set a date for the next session.

Well, as I feared, the next session was not to be. I came down with an awful cold that quickly morphed into a persistent bronchitis. The next time I saw my trainer, she was peering around my front door thrusting food sent by the ladies of our Bible study group into my hands and refusing to enter my home for fear of catching what I had. I looked at her ruefully and said, "See what I told you? Something always stops my exercise programs."

Shaking my head, I retreated to my family room to resume my prone position on the sofa. I had been having sleepless nights filled with violent coughing episodes that sometimes caused me to throw up and grab at my head that at times felt like it would explode.

My days, therefore, found me propped up on the sofa trying to grant my body the few hours of the sleep it had been denied. From that position, I filled my days with YouTube videos.

That's when I stumbled upon the interview with War Room lead actress, Priscilla Shirer, our beloved Bible Study writer and teacher. As is the custom with YouTube, the videos skipped from one to the other following the trend of the previous topic. That practice led me to make a discovery. Priscilla Shirer, our favorite Bible Study presenter, was also a talk show host! Who knew!

As the videos progressed, she had moved from interviewee to interviewer! Her guest was a slender, middle-aged blonde with a peculiar accent, who spoke with passion about the brain, and, in particular, the concept of neuroplasticity.

Now in full disclosure, the brain and its working were never an interest of mine, but Dr Caroline Leaf, neuroscientist and Christian minister, relayed her information in such a manner that I was riveted. Before I knew it, I was enrolled in "Brain School," as the video stream deserted Priscilla and segued to back-to-back sessions with Dr Leaf.

Sadly, I was also extremely weak and breathless. The Bible study group faithfully sent meals to our home, aware that I was too weak to prepare them. I needed to be helped upstairs every night. My many visits to my family doctor and the pulmonologist plus myriad medicines and treatments did very little to alleviate my suffering. I was so ill, I noticed I was beginning to drag my right leg as I walked. Eventually I concluded I must be allergic to something in my highly treed neighborhood.

Jonathan had completed a year of college in Panama and would head out in a few months to complete his studies abroad. Jason was already in the US at college. Jovanna was in her junior year in high school. Selwyn was away on a business trip. So, desperate for relief, I had Jonathan drive me to our home by the beach to spend the weekend. The difference was startling. I felt revived and finally began to breathe and sleep well.

When Sunday evening came, I begged to be left there while my family returned to their commitments in the city. They refused to leave me there alone, and worse, without a car. We agreed that, as soon as Selwyn arrived later in the week, we would return.

I returned home, and so did the cough, as soon as we neared my neighborhood. I could not wait for the weekend to arrive. I would retreat to the beach once again for much-needed relief. As Friday finally rolled around, I planned to head straight there.

In order to beat the usual horrendous traffic, we would get Jovanna, as soon as school was out at 3p.m. and keep going. Mid-plan, she reminded me that that evening was her school's basketball night. She would need to attend. Not daunted, we decided to make the trip at 9:00pm when the games ended. At 9 p.m. I received a call from my husband lamenting the snaking traffic that was still wending its way past the school in the direction of the beach. No worries, we would leave at 11. Surely by then it would be smooth sailing.

Already weakened, I climbed into bed planning to get up later for the trip. Both our children decided they were not really keen on going and opted to stay home. Selwyn and I finally decided that, given all the changes and the lateness of the hour, we would ourselves turn in for the night and leave very early in the morning for the beach. That night, Friday the 13th of October, 2017, was the last time I felt fully in control of all my limbs. At 1 a.m. on Saturday October 14, my world, as I had known it, ended.

55

Life Changes

Sometime about 1 a.m. I attempt to roll out of bed to head to the bathroom. That's when I feel it. There is the distinct sensation of a giant snake wiggling around in my bed. The even stranger thing is that I cannot locate my right arm, as I am attempting to prop myself up. The sensation I feel could best be described as a writhing, frozen, electrical shock. And my right arm is unresponsive.

More precisely, I can't find it. Alarmed, I call for Selwyn to help get me to a standing position. I feel fine except that my right arm, which I can see is there now that the light has been turned on, is totally unresponsive. I make a dash to the standing mirror in our room and begin to do the stroke tests I had often read about:

Is my face twisted? No

Can I stick my tongue straight out? Yes

Do I have a headache? No

Can I say my name clearly? Yes

Is everything else working? Yes

Good! This was not a stroke, I reassured myself. But what was it?

In no time Selwyn was dressed and helping me into clothes, so we could head to the ER. Usually when we are needing care at Hospital Nacional, we would first make a call to our family pediatrician Dr Medrano. He would alert whichever specialist we would need to see when we got there. This time, however, that completely escaped our minds.

As we rolled up to the door of the ER, and I was whisked inside in a wheelchair, I was filled with confusion. I was in no pain whatsoever, but my right arm was still not listening to me nor obeying my commands.

I quickly got myself registered, and the doctor on call began the preliminary testing. The conclusion was that whatever was the matter seemed to be connected to my nervous system. Coincidentally, the doctor exclaimed, there was a neurosurgeon still in the hospital at that late hour. This was highly unusual, she noted, after she called him to have a look at me.

As I lay on the small bed in the ER's brightly lit examining room, I heard voices and saw the privacy screen being pulled open. I was greeted by a pleasant young man, maybe in his late 30's, who first looked at my file then asked if Thompson was my surname.

Though I was on the verge of celebrating my 35th wedding anniversary that December and had long adopted the Batchelor surname, in the Panamanian health system, I am still Diane Thompson. Panama has a system of naming that never discards the maiden name. That practice turned out to be for my benefit.

Coincidentally, this kindly young doctor was also a Thompson. And his name, Daniel, happened to be the name of one of my favorite nephews. (In case you're curious, all my nephews are my favorites.) His warm bedside manner combined with our "familial" ties put me at ease. As he talked soothingly and easily, he was carrying out his own physical examination. When he was through, he suggested I undergo radiographic tests to rule out a stroke, but thought that, given my history, I was more than likely just suffering from a pinched nerve. Selwyn is now convinced that he said that just to put me at ease, for when I suggested that there was then no need to do the brain scan, he insisted it was a necessity.

Given the fact that I was quite lucid, had absolutely no head pain, no slurred speech, had clear vision, I was totally unprepared for what the results revealed. Even as I was engaged in conversation with my congenial doctor, there was blood on my brain. The results confirmed his suspicion that I had experienced the rupture of a blood vessel. He was able to confirm from the images that it was associated with a very uncommon congenital brain malformation he called an AVM. The results showed an Arteriovenous Malformation. There it was in black, white, and varying shades of grey—I was never completely right in the head! (My children will get a kick out of that one.)

The disease usually causes problems such as seizures, headaches, as well as stroke-like symptoms. I had never experienced any of those. This condition had gone unde-tected for over 57 years! All these many years later, after an extended period of violent coughing, it had finally ruptured and affected only my right arm.

My doctor, whom I soon "adopted" as my brother, mar-veled that my arm was the only thing affected, given the location of the bleed. Apparently, I could have lost speech, vision, mobility...the list went on. I could have died.

I was overwhelmed at the thought. I had been born with this condition. It had been an explosive mine waiting for the inadvertent contact that would have been sure to wreak havoc and even death. This thought became more focused, as Selwyn relayed to me his brother's comment.

Selwyn's brother, a surgeon of many years, on hearing of my hemorrhage had exclaimed, "What a good thing it was that Diane didn't have children naturally!" He had seen not one, but two colleagues die in childbirth, only to realize afterwards that they both had the same malformation as me. Look at GOD!

The strangest thing then happened to me. I was being admitted to the semi-intensive care unit of the hospital with blood on my brain and an arm that hung limp, yet I was awash with an inexplicable peace. I had absolutely no fear of dying. I finally understood what the King James Bible meant in Philippians 4:7 by "Peace that passeth all understanding." This was amazing. I was not afraid!

My first thought was to make sure no one else was alarmed when they heard the news, so I grabbed my cell phone and wrote a quick note making sure that first, they knew I was fine, then that I was in the hospital. Despite that, my friend Flory made it to the hospital that night even before I was transferred from the ER.

The next few days were a blur. I met technicians, sub-specialists and, for the first time in my life, a male nurse. Somehow my bronchitis disappeared in the hospital, and I was finally able to catch up on all the rest I had missed during the previous month.

Between my many hours of drug-induced sleep, I seem to have been party to numerous decisions concerning the way forward. I found myself in a sea of words and phrases that made me feel like I had migrated to another planet. "The lesion is near the motor strip. It measures 2.5 cm x 0.7 cm x 0.8 cm. Venous drainage is superficial. This is consistent with a Spetzler Martin grade 2." What did all that mean?

From conversations with my "brother-doctor" I learn that the malformation is too deep in my brain for surgery to be considered. That's because the location of the AVM is very close to the area controlling motor and sensation on my right side. Based on its location, it is considered inoperable. Instead they suggest a process called embolization. "Embolization is filling the nidus with a glue-like substance to occlude the rogue veins." I hope you understood this strange language which, all too quickly, I was being forced to decipher. I won't even try to translate for you. How about I let you join me on the adventure into my head instead?

But first let me have Selwyn take a stab at explaining why we chose to do what we did.

"From the moment of diagnosis, I knew we had to make a decision as to whether or not we should go ahead with the surgical procedure. Both options had risks.

"To not go ahead meant Diane would be walking normally, as soon as the blood receded from her brain, and she would probably use her right arm reasonably well. But the chances of another bleed in her brain would always be there. A second bleed increases the possibility of death by 40%, or if not death, she could suffer really bad deficits like not walking, not talking, or not being able to use one of her hands."

"The second option was to do the procedure, but if it did not go well, while the possibility of death would be reduced, all of the really bad deficits could show up."

Did that help? I don't blame you, if it didn't. The long and the short of it was that we decided to risk the embolization.

So, decision made, after a day of tests they took me to the operating room where I was placed on a hard table, which seemed to be, itself, some sort of machine. Another machine loomed above my head and the vascular neurosurgeon stood to the side holding something like a wand and casting glances at a video screen nearby. My neurosurgeon was also there, and truthfully, I can't recall who else. What I do recall is their having to secure my way-ward right arm, so it wouldn't fall off the bed. Who knew my brain controlled my resting arm!

They clamped my head between a donut-shaped cushion and a band across my forehead. This was to ensure that I didn't move while they were inside my head. Would you move if someone were inserting a probe into your brain? I didn't think so either.

They then administered a needle with a local anesthesia into my leg just below my groin. I felt a lot of pressure on my upper thigh, as they began to insert a thin piece of equipment. This, I'm told, is the catheter with the camera, which would allow the surgeons to see exactly where the malformation lay within my brain. By now, I hope you realize that, in the meantime, I was fully awake and trying not to freak out at the thought of something foreign travelling up into my body to roam around inside my brain.

Being awake, I could see sporadic flashes of light and at times feel sharp stabs of pain. They were moving around inside my brain! I could hear the conversation above my head, as the surgeons examined the images the camera was sending them. They sounded confident. I didn't detect alarm. That was good. I began to relax. Then it was over.

The surgeon removed the probe from my thigh and warned me not to move the leg for some hours, since they had gone through a major artery and didn't want to risk bleeding. That could be fatal. I was returned to my bed in the semi-intensive care unit, and they proceeded to give me a bedpan. I was no longer free to move to the bathroom by myself.

And I did mention the male nurse, right? It doesn't help that they recommended that I drink a lot of fluid to flush the dye used to highlight the area for such a procedure. After a while, I forgot to be embarrassed. As they say, "A girl's gotta do what a girl's gotta do." So, I did.

The good news is that after the required number of hours, I was able to move my right leg and again help myself to the bathroom. Oh joy! The things I had previously taken for granted.

I was required to wait one more day, before they would perform the embolization. This time, instead of dye, they would disperse a glue-like substance into the malformed veins in the hopes that they would eventually die off, and the blood to my brain would be diverted to pass through more appropriate vessels. Something like that. As you may guess I flunked the language course of that strange planet.

After the intervening day, I was ready to get the embolization underway. I was just a bit more relaxed, yet because I was more aware of the huge risks associated with the procedure, I was also a bit apprehensive. Very strange bedfellows, don't you think? But such was my reality. Once again, it was the peace that most made its presence felt. I felt safe no matter what.

Owing to a backlog of procedures that day, mine, which had been scheduled for morning, was delayed till the afternoon. As they wheeled me towards the surgery, the smiling faces of Isa and Flory, two dear friends from our church, greeted me. This was a special reminder that our GOD loved and cared for us. Those ladies provided a needed break for Selwyn. He was living a nightmare. Their pleasant chatter was the distraction he needed, while the doctors again entered my head.

They entered my brain through the same opening they had made before in my leg. Once again, I saw the flashes of light and felt the stabs of pain. My right arm was once again strapped to the bed to prevent it from falling. But there was a glimmer of hope. Just before the procedure, I began to feel a tiny bit more control there.

When the procedure was complete, the doctors seemed satisfied that they had managed to fill at least 90% of the malformation with the glue. If all went well, I would soon be free of the malady of which I had been unaware all these many years.

When I was returned to my bed in the semi-intensive care unit, it was again with the warning not to move my right leg. I kept it motionless till the next morning. When I was finally given the go-ahead to move it, nothing happened. By that I mean my leg did not respond. I was unable to lift it.

My doctor visited later in the day and reassured me that this was possibly a reaction to the blood that may have been relocated when the glue was introduced into the rogue veins. After all, the original bleed had been in a very precarious position and it was a wonder I had not originally suffered more deficiencies than just my right arm. He also believed there might still have been some swelling after the procedure. He expected that, as soon as the swelling resolved, I would be regaining more use of my leg.

Remember that male nurse? It turns out he was also a believer and had a lovely singing voice. Before I left the semi-intensive care unit, I had the joy of having him stand by my bedside and serenade me with a beautiful song of worship. (Ah, the little gifts!)

And remember the YouTube videos with Dr Caroline Leaf? My doctor confirmed what I had learnt from her— that I could expect my brain to eventually make new connections through a process called neuroplasticity. That was one word that didn't need explaining. I had already learnt it weeks before in her "Brain School." My FATHER had been preparing me. In the meantime, I would enjoy the crazy peace.

56

I Believe in GOD, the FATHER

I was soon transferred to my own hospital room, away from the plethora of machines and tubes. The spirit of peace continued to envelop me. I was grateful for a room with a window, a sofa bed where Selwyn could sleep, and a private bathroom. I was also grateful that I could now freely play music without disturbing anyone. My anthem became Chevelle Franklin's *No Foreign God*. As I worshipped, the penny dropped. The scales fell from my eyes, and I could finally see.

For years I had embraced GOD's selfie—JESUS. I had enjoyed HIM as the HOLY SPIRIT. But GOD, the FATHER was not relatable to me. That day, as I lay on my hospital bed, I finally began to understand and embrace GOD as FATHER. Actually, it had begun the year my own father died. My heart had then begun to see GOD the FATHER through different eyes.

However, that day in the hospital was when I truly began to grasp what my HEAVENLY DADDY had been doing all those years ago when HE had denied me children at an early age. And I was completely overwhelmed with gratitude.

I was 36 years old when I became pregnant with our first son. That made me a "mature primigravida" at his conception. In case you're wondering, that's another one of those words from the other planet. This one translated simply meant "old woman first pregnancy."

I remember strongly disagreeing with my obstetrician when he insisted that I had to have a cesarean section. He argued that my age was a factor of concern, and in addition, being a friend and being very aware of how long it had taken us to conceive, he was taking no chances.

I was not having it. This was a fight I would win. After all this was my body, and I was not going to be denied the perfectly natural experience of bringing my child into the world.

I recall sitting with a colleague at work one day before heading out to one of my final obstetrician appointments. His wife had given birth to a baby only a few months before. In casual conversation I asked how the baby was doing. His demeanor instantly changed. He sadly reported that the baby appeared to be brain damaged and possibly blind in one eye. He explained that this was owing to complications during natural delivery. Although they had eventually been forced to do a C-section, it had come too late.

I realized GOD was speaking to me. I drove from the Palisadoes Strip oblivious of the sparkling blue Caribbean Sea that gently caressed its shores. Lost in thought, I made it through the bustle of New Kingston with its mini-high-rises, and arrived at my Tangerine Place appointment. This was the conclusion I drew from my restless thoughts:

What was important was not how my baby came into the world.

More important was that my baby was whole and healthy.

With that, I parked my car, and waddled up the stairs to Dr Daley's office.

When it was my turn, I entered his consultation room. As usual, his radio was streaming beautiful music. He offered me a warm greeting and seemed to prepare himself for us to continue the "Battle of the Birth." Taking a deep breath, he ventured, "We would like to schedule the C-section for..." I don't remember the date. It didn't matter. I was now prepared to do whatever he said. When my response was a simple, "OK," you could see the shock register on his face. It took him a while to realize that I was actually agreeing to have my child by C-section. By the time he got used to this new paradigm, I had already fished out my agenda and had the date noted.

As it turns out, Jonathan did try to come naturally. I had been having a week of Braxton Hicks contractions (false labor), when one Friday something strange occurred. I was on leave and alone at home in our apartment. Suddenly after a fairly mild contraction, I passed a strange gooey object. Selwyn was out of phone contact, so I immediately called my friend Janice, who rushed over to get me to the hospital. Between phone calls to her and the doctor, I ascertained that I had had something called "the show." This was the first sign of an imminent labor. My baby was on its way! This was two weeks before my scheduled C-section. I secretly hoped that I would have my baby naturally after all.

Well, that was not to be. Selwyn arrived shortly after I got to the hospital. He stood at the door, as my doctor whisked me into the operating theatre. I recognized the anesthetist as a girl from my high school. I recall a sensation like my belly and back had firmly shaken hands, then I was sedated. The next time I awoke, I was the mother of a beautiful baby boy who, in spite of his large eyes that my sister claimed as hers, looked just like his dad.

All my three children were delivered by C-section. For years I regretted that, and I am now ashamed to admit how often I whined about it after every incident of pain from the surgeries' after-effects. I called my FATHER mean. HE had to be if HE could allow me to suffer so much.

As I lay in my hospital bed bathed in the music of Chevelle Franklin's *No Foreign God*, I remembered again the first thing my surgeon brother-in-law had exclaimed— how fortunate it was that I had never delivered naturally. How fortunate it was that I had been made to wait. Instead of withholding blessing from me in the mean time, and causing me to live with pain, my loving FATHER had been saving my life!

After all those years, I was reminded of the birthday where my dad's tender love had been on display for me. And as an added bonus, the birthday gift if you would, the

AVM affected my right arm. Guess what? I was born left-handed!! What a thoughtful DAD!!

As I did to my earthly dad, so I did to my HEAVENLY FATHER. I apologized for ever doubting HIS love. And like my dad, HE embraced me and let me know all was forgiven. My mean time was GOD working in the mean-time.

57

Fearfully and Wonderfully Made?

As I spent the rest of my time in hospital between sleep and worship, I began to piece together another tiny bit of the puzzle that was my life. Psalm 139 had become a favorite chapter of mine when, wrapped in the folly of youth, I had complained that I didn't like how I looked. I began to pray for the LORD to make me beautiful. I cannot even now recall the flaw that caused me to think I was not beautiful to look at. (How youth is wasted on the young!) I look back at that precious, lovely young woman and wonder if I had needed glasses. But the LORD took advantage of my questioning to carefully minister the words of that Psalm to me. The lesson I learnt from my stupidity was this:

I was fearfully and wonderfully made.

The LORD knit me together in my mother's womb. (Let that sink in. Knitting is very intentional—the colors, the stitches, the design.)

Everything about me was made to glorify HIM. Everything.

"Even this, GOD?" I asked in disbelief. The Psalm had again come to confront me. "YOU knit a malformation into my brain when I was being formed in my mother's womb!" The idea is chilling. How could that have been a part of HIS plan for me?

As I wrestled with this thought, the peace that made no sense continued to fill my heart and mind.

Since that time, I have looked back on the many opportunities for encouraging others that my illness has caused. I now agree with Katherine Wolf that my pain has become my platform. That's what HE knitted into me—an opportunity for HIS amazing love to be on glorious display.

58

HIS Manifold Wisdom

Thanks to another insurance plan, I was able to have the services of 24-hour nursing care while I was in my hospital room. I still needed to be helped to do everything. The morning after I was transferred, two days after my procedure, I decided to try my legs again.

On the first day, I had noticed I was unable to sense my foot making contact with the floor. The next morning, however, when I was helped out of bed, I felt my toes grab the floor. Encouraged, I asked the nurse to stand close by, but allow me to try walking on my own. As one shaky step led to another, I became ecstatic with gratitude. I grabbed my phone and asked my nurse to film me walking from my bed to the bathroom and back. I made it unaided. It was a moment of triumph.

The video, originally meant for only my husband and children, soon reached my brothers and sister, then some close friends, at which point it took on a life of its own. It was being shared everywhere. I didn't mind. I was just so happy that I was getting my leg back. Look at GOD!

Now you may remember my confusion as to how GOD could have purposely put a malformation into me? Well, I was beginning to formulate an answer. And it was as simple as it was complex.

My life is for GOD's glory. Ephesians 3:10 in the Amplified Bible says:

"So now through the church the multifaceted wisdom of God [in all its countless aspects] might now be made known [revealing the mystery] to the [angelic] rulers and authorities in the heavenly places."

GOD was using my little, insignificant life to show off big time to the spiritual rulers and authorities in a realm I could only imagine but not fully comprehend. Of one thing I was sure. That was the only realm that really mattered.

As I lay in worship on my bed, I also began to recall some of the things GOD had spoken to me over the years. I knew HE had a plan for our families, but as many would agree, that is always the hardest ground to till. We had prayed many years for our families, but feared that, ever so often, we ourselves had turned them away from a deeper seeking of the LORD.

So, imagine my shock and incredulous delight when I received the following message from my sister:

> *I've been watching your video over and over Diane. My first reaction if I'm honest was despair as I was shaken by the fact that you were so affected in your mobility that what I was looking at was something you were so happy about. As I kept watching and got over the initial shock I was then moved by your gratitude and joy in the midst of it all. You have always been an inspiration to us all my sister but I do believe you've surpassed yourself this time. What a testimony of God's grace and even more so what an example you are to us as individuals. Smile on your face like a kid at Christmas. No moaning. No feeling sorry for yourself. You're a true legend. I'm so proud to call you my sister.* 🖤🖤🖤🖤

I couldn't believe my eyes. This was my heartfelt response:

Oh wow! You're trying to make a grown woman bawl! I hear stuff like this from people who don't know me really well and it slides off of me like ingratiating flattery. But to hear that from you...my own sister, who has seen my insides out, means more than I could ever express. Thank you!! ♥♥♥

I also looked up to my DADDY, and I whispered, "Thank YOU!" HE has a plan. I get to participate. How amazingly awesome!

59

Houston, We Have a Problem

After leaving the hospital, I needed daily nursing care. At first, I needed to be wheeled around in a wheelchair then I used a walker, and finally a cane.

I had to move into a makeshift bedroom downstairs.

I needed to borrow a child's bed rail to make sure I wouldn't fall off the bed.

I couldn't keep my arm stationary on any surface. It would flop down.

I experienced uncontrollable shaking when trying to do simple movement with my arm.

I lost feeling in sections of my right arm.

A flat surface felt like it was corrugated.

I gave "ghost hugs"—My hand and upper arm felt present, but my forearm was absent.

Eventually as feeling returned, the signals were mixed up. Cotton balls felt excruciatingly uncomfortable when they touched my skin.

My entire right arm felt like it belonged to the comic book superhero, The Thing.

The gentlest pressure was unbearable

My sense of distance was messed up, as things on my right side appeared to be nearer than they were.

I could not walk a straight line, and

I learnt big words like proprioception, neuropathic pain, algology, and vascular neurosurgeon.

After two months of excellent physiotherapy in Panama, I was able to regain quite a bit of my right-limb functions. However, I eventually began to plateau in my progress. That's when I decided to make use of the insurance benefit that allowed us to access care from some of the best treatment centers in the US.

Despite my progress, I still needed help for quite a few ordinary tasks. Taking to the service providers' website, we began scrolling through the various states, mentally reviewing our options for each one. We came up with a blank.

At the time I was doing therapy four times a week. I still had a nurse accompanying me, and Bible Study friends who took turns picking me up from therapy each day. I would need a lot of hands-on care. That was a lot to ask of anyone. We gave up on the idea.

A few weeks later, we again decided to search for overseas therapy options. I was still unable to walk unaided. This time I did an online search for the "best therapy centers." I would go by state. As I inputted my search criteria, up popped a hospital then ranked as the number two in the USA and number one in Texas. It was located in Houston, and was called TIRR Memorial Hermann. I had never heard about this hospital, but I knew that Houston had a reputation for excellent medical care.

More significant to me, though, was that a very dear friend of mine, Becky, had not long before returned to Houston to set up home there. I knew I could count on her to help me in time of need. I just needed to see how near her home was to the hospital. After all, Texas was the big, wide state.

When I checked, I discovered there was only 40-minutes' distance between her home in the suburbs and the hospital in the city. I could manage that commute. So, I first told her that I was fine with a "no," and then I asked her to discuss with her family the idea of a disabled me living with them for a few months.

Without hesitation, she declared that I was more than welcome to follow up my treatment from her home. I insisted she speak to her family before deciding. In a few minutes, she called back to say it was settled. I should book my ticket to come and stay at her home. In no time all the arrangements were made, and I found myself at the airport, seated in a wheelchair, saying goodbye to my husband and daughter headed for follow-up in Houston.

In the interim between my first introduction to the hospital and my leaving Panama, I had discovered that the hospital had satellite therapy centers. It turns out that they had only recently opened a center in Sugarland, and it was only 13 minutes away from Becky's home! It was so recently opened that even though it was nearby, she had never even seen it before. Look at GOD!

In my initial assessment meetings with the Houston professionals, I continued to hear a similar refrain:

Surprise at how well I was doing in such a short period,
Respect for the medical professionals who had cared
for me in Panama, and

Shock that, given the location of the malformation, I had suffered so few deficits.

I can still recall the tears that welled up in the eyes of the speech therapist who evaluated me. She couldn't help remarking how astounding it was that I had suffered no impediment in my speech or cognitive abilities considering the location of the malformation and the area of the bleed.

After three weeks of being in Houston and a week of therapy at the center, I was able to walk without the use of the cane I had brought with me from Panama. On one marvelous occasion, when my son, Jonathan, visited me there during his Spring Break, I even found myself running next to him along a beautiful tree-lined avenue in downtown Houston.

Because of the AVM I had been denied the joy of helping Jonathan settle into his apartment, when in January he had moved to the U.S. to complete his college education. And here I was now in March, on my own two feet, spending a whole day exploring Houston with him. I felt like a gleeful child!

Sharing a home with Becky and her family was also priceless. In no time her church family became mine. Some of them even helped transport me to and from therapy sessions. The warmth and graciousness that enveloped me from start to finish played a key part in my healing (the awesome Indian cooking, the movie afternoons with the "Juniors" (her beautiful girls), the bubble tea dates, and so much more). Becky's graciousness even extended to her welcoming Selwyn and Jovanna, who came to spend some precious days with me during Panama's Carnival holidays.

A "JESUS kiss" (to borrow a phrase) was that Kristy, a lovely woman I had met in Panama Ladies Bible Study, just happened to live minutes away from Becky's home. She committed to overseeing my in-home exercises and accompanied me to all my hospital consultation visits. The laughter we shared during our time together was its own medicine.

Another Panama Houston friend, Alisha, faithfully transported me to her Ladies' Bible Study in the city every week. I met and fellowshipped with so many lovely women, the sisters I had not met before. The love and care lavished on me by my JESUS family in Houston is a gift for which I will be forever grateful.

After two months I was able to return home, no longer dropping things from my right hand, walking with just a very slight limp, and able to tackle most of the normal everyday necessities of life. I have since been able to travel, do walking tours, and even run from train, to tube, and through an airport in order to catch my flight home. Sometimes I even manage heels!

60

HE's Still Working on Me

On the surface I really do not show any deficits, though I continue to do physiotherapy, especially on my right arm. I have good strength on both sides. The feeling in my right arm and hand has been compromised by the bleed. At times I have significant shoulder pain, though I can still do most things. These are the remnants that cause me never to forget:

Most days I struggle with pain.

I have shoulder pain.

I have numb, painful fingers.

I have to look to make sure my right hand is making contact with an object.

I have to be careful of getting my fingers caught and damaged.

I sometimes drop stuff.

I deal with sensations of a frozen right arm.

I startle easily (much to the delight of my daughter who was always chagrined that she couldn't easily succeed at scaring me.)

Things seem much nearer on my right side, so I'm a very nervous passenger in a car. (Amazingly I am a much better driver than passenger.)

I have swollen feet, especially on my right side.

The toes on my right foot are still stiff.

Walking normally takes much effort and concentration. Sometimes I struggle to maintain my balance.

I call myself Weather Woman, because on overcast days I suffer from strange headaches, and a sense of carrying around twice my weight on one side. It seems I'm sensitive to a change in barometric pressure. This leads to many days filled with deep fatigue.

Why have I catalogued this long list of issues, you may ask? It's because most of this is invisible to those with whom I interact. I've taken to calling it "my personal business," since very few people know or even need to know about this. I am learning, though, that my experience is so similar to most humans.

As my dear friend Kristy wisely quipped one day, "Most of us compare our insides with other people's outsides." We each carry secret pains, some of them physical, a host of them emotional. They are the residual effects of trauma of some kind. For some of us it's more obvious than others. But to all of them HE says, "My grace is sufficient for you [My lovingkindness and My mercy are more than enough—always available—regardless of the situation]; for [My] power is being perfected [and is completed and shows itself most effectively] in [your] weakness" (2 Corinthians 12: AMP).

Brawta

Kintsugi

roken pottery mended with a precious metal. That's what this Japanese word means. I have come to see that GOD has melded HIMSELF into my broken spaces creating a precious masterpiece of HIS own design. I am truly beginning to grasp that my broken-ness (my mean times) is my blessing. I get to be the backdrop against which GOD's glory shines.

...we have this precious treasure [the good news about salvation] in [unworthy] earthen vessels [of human frailty],

311

so that the grandeur and surpassing greatness of the power will be [shown to be] from God

[His sufficiency] and not from ourselves.

We are pressured in every way [hedged in], but not crushed;

perplexed [unsure of finding a way out],

but not driven to despair;

hunted down and persecuted,

but not deserted [to stand alone];

struck down,

but never destroyed;

always carrying around in the body the dying of Jesus,

so that the [resurrection] life of Jesus also may be shown in our body.

Therefore, we do not become discouraged [spiritless, disappointed, or afraid].

Though our outer self is [progressively] wasting away,

yet our inner self is being [progressively] renewed day by day.

For our momentary,

light distress [this passing trouble]

is producing for us an eternal weight of glory

[a fullness] beyond all measure [surpassing all comparisons,

a transcendent splendor and an endless blessedness]!
So we look not at the things which are seen,
but at the things which are unseen; for the things which
are visible are temporal
[just brief and fleeting],
but the things which are invisible are everlasting and
imperishable" (2 Corinthians 4:7-10, 16-18 AMP).

"Therefore, I will all the more gladly boast in my weaknesses, so that the power of Christ [may completely enfold me and] may dwell in me" 2 Cor. 12:9 AMP).

In February, 2019, tests at Johns Hopkins showed that the AVM is reduced in size thanks to the embolization, but it is still there. They feel it has shrunk significantly enough to restore my risk factor to what it was before the bleed. They recommend cyber knife (a radiation treatment) to partially obliterate it.

However, after regaining 90% functionality, never having had a seizure nor prolonged headaches, and functioning without medication, I'm hesitant to do further treatment. There's more. They also say that at my "young age" (No laughing allowed!) there is a risk of developing brain cancer from the radiation further down the road.

My doctor in Panama, after reviewing my results, agrees with my decision to not do radiation treatment of the malformation. We have agreed to doing periodic six-month, then annual checks to ensure that the malformation isn't growing or developing aneurysms. I thank GOD for this, and will continue therapy to keep regaining strength and normal function on my right side.

I am beginning to realize that, before I was born GOD had tucked a love note into my brain. It was one of those "Do not open till..." It was in the form of an AVM. Through this malformation I have come to grasp the depth of my FATHER's love for me that no perfect day has ever been able to convey. Through it I am being propelled further into purpose—HIS purpose for me.

I also thank GOD that through this hard experience in my life (this mean time), I have come to embrace a group of fellow travelers who all suffer from brain AVMs as well as AVMs in other parts of the body. We have become the family we never knew we had. We grieve with each other and we rejoice with each other. Like my 21-year old self at the concert tightly gripping Janet's hand, we hold each other up, as we step onto the world's stage. We know we are not alone. We wait in hope.

Epilogue

In the meantime, I have been swept up in a wave of gratitude to my FATHER for HIS gift of life to me. As I said, it makes no sense. But now I understand that it is truly in our weakness that HIS great strength shines through.

One of the people whose story greatly impacted my life has been a young woman who, in her early 20's and just six months after the birth of her baby, suffered a major stroke. It was as a result of the very same malformation with which I was born. In truth, before discovering mine, I had never before heard of such a thing. And here is where my loving FATHER shines through once more. The very first time I encountered another human being with this malformation, it was listening to Jay and Katherine Wolf being interviewed about the stroke that left her in a wheelchair.

I had seen her being interviewed before. It could even have been somewhere during the time just prior the discovery of my AVM. But in the same way that you never notice red cars till you've just purchased one, I totally missed the reason for her disability. Her story, however, was riveting, and her joy and peace undeniable. She drew me in.

Some time after the discovery of my AVM, I came across this tragically beautiful couple once again being interviewed. As I listened and looked at the images being flashed across the screen, there was a jolt of familiarity that set me upright and grabbed my attention. Did she also have an AVM?! Sure enough, that was what had exploded her brain and left her with so many disabilities. As I grieved for her, I also felt a strong kinship with this young family.

This connection was permanently forged when I recently passed through a period of consistent pain and discomfort in my right arm. Nearly two years had passed. I had weaned myself off the many opioids that did little more than mask the pain for a short while before demanding a higher dosage providing progressively less relief.

I grappled with desperation at the thought that I seemed to be doomed to live a life of pain. Even though I had not lost my hope or trust in the LORD, I struggled with a deep tiredness. I was literally sick and tired of living in constant pain.

Many people who had witnessed my joy and peace at the outset of my illness, felt the need to encourage me to be joyful in the midst of my discomfort. I began to feel like it would be best to tell my sadness only to JESUS and my husband Selwyn. Acknowledging my pain made others noticeably uncomfortable.

We recently spent time in Atlanta with some dear friends, en route to settling our daughter into college. Our friends, Karl and Marcia, invited us to visit their church that weekend. I had hit a crisis in my search for pain relief and had cried myself to sleep. In the midst of this turmoil, I was again blessed to receive a gift from my loving FATHER.

That Sunday morning at Passion City Church, I was awash in healing tears. Instead of Louie Giglio, as I had expected, it was Jay and Katherine Wolf who sat on stage to share. They may have been addressing the whole church, but I was receiving a personal message from my FATHER. HE assured me it was OK to live in "peace with a profound sense of loss" and that "there's good in the hard and hard in the good." I was reminded that I could "hope it forward."

That's what I needed to remember. I could grieve my loss and mourn my pain all the while fully trusting in my good FATHER and his good plans for me. That's what JESUS did in Gethsemane. I could have hope in the midst of pain and offer that hope to others who, like me, may be experiencing a mean time. Even though it's hard, "there's good in the hard." I get to join my FATHER in HIS work of loving people back to HIM.

> He comforts us in all our troubles so that we can comfort others.
> When they are troubled, we will be able to give them the same comfort God has given us.
> For the more we suffer for Christ, the more God will shower us with his comfort through Christ (2 Corinthians 1:4-5, NLT).

These mean times have become the heavy tools that have been added to my tool belt. I've now embraced a different perspective on what it means to have baggage. Our pain, stresses and trauma do create baggage. But it's not a negative thing. I do have baggage—a bag full of tools, so that I'm equipped to comfort others with the same comfort I have received from my FATHER.

"Even when we are weighed down with troubles, it is for your comfort and salvation! For when we ourselves are comforted, we will certainly comfort you. Then you can patiently endure the same things we suffer" (2 Corinthians 1:6, NLT).

Now that's hoping it forward. Let's be clear. I don't do a jig when I pass through mean times. But I do remain in peace, and I'm filled with expectation of the big reveal of the masterpiece my FATHER is so painstakingly crafting. I'm trusting HIS heart, when I can't trace HIS hand. Even when I don't see it. HE's working! And with my tool belt tightly strapped on and weighing me down, I get to join HIM in HIS work.

"But as for me, I will sing of Your mighty strength and power; Yes, I will sing joyfully of Your lovingkindness in the morning; For You have been my stronghold and a refuge in the day of my distress" (Psalms 59:16, AMP).

Acknowledgments

A book is born when you can no longer ignore the voices that call you to write. For some the voice calls from deep within. For others the voice they hear stares at them in familiar faces. This book is the response to many who through the years have urged me to write.

My precious family—and the friends who have been family to me—I don't deserve you. I thank GOD for each and every one of you.

Brownie Lee, my high school English teacher, you were the first to see my potential and demand good writing from me. You made a 70% feel like an A. Thank you for setting the bar high and teaching me the value of constructive feedback.

Dinorah Blackman, you were the straw that broke the camel's back. Thanks for relentlessly urging me to write. Happy now?

Deborah Henry Coplin, you challenged me to go beyond simply telling a story. You dared me to become a writer. Ok. I know I have not arrived. I thank GOD for your footprint on my rear end.

Josett Peat, cuz, you are the maximum. I love that we're joined by blood. Thanks for the hours of proofreading and editing with me way before I even truly understood what those words meant.

Kwame Dawes, through you, my Aba has continued to mother me. I cannot thank you enough. You took the trepidation out of the process, and made me believe I could actually do this. Your kind, but honest feedback has helped shape this entire work. Thank you!

My team: Marci Loewen, Sharon Knight, Anthea Edalere Henderson, Nicole Bain, Debra Duncker Davis, Elspeth (and Genesis) Madden, Samantha Cowan, Alison Otway, Ruth Taylor, Jonathan and Jovanna Batchelor, THANK YOU! Your feedback and practical suggestions were invaluable.

Made in the USA
Columbia, SC
15 July 2021

41900347R00207